Building Reading Comprehension

High-Interest Selections for Critical Reading Skills

Written by
Gail Blasser Rile

Cover Illustration by
Matthew Van Zomeren

Inside Illustrations by
Shauna Mooney Kawasaki

Published by Instructional Fair • TS Denison
an imprint of

 **McGraw-Hill
Children's Publishing**

About the Author

Gail Blasser Riley, an award-winning author, has written more than 200 books, articles, poems, and greeting verses for adults and children of all ages. Her publications include more than two dozen leveled readers, as well as articles for children's writers. Riley has taught classes from the preschool through graduate levels, and she frequently writes and edits educational material. Riley visits classrooms across the country to share her work. Gail Blasser Riley's accomplishments and awards include a book on the Reading Recovery List, a Children's Book Council Notable Children's Trade Book in the Field of Social Studies, a New York Public Library Book for the Teen Age, a Young Adult Library Services Association's Quick Picks nomination, and a children's book recommended by the Los Angeles Times. Riley, who is also an attorney, has served as Regional Advisor for the Society of Children's Book Writers and Illustrators. She is co-author of their "Directory Guide to Educational Markets."

Credits

Author: Gail Blasser Riley
Cover Artist: Matthew Van Zomeren
Inside Illustrations: Shauna Mooney Kawasaki
Project Director/Editor: Elizabeth Flikkema
Editors: Sara Bierling, Alyson Kieda
Graphic Layout: Tracy L. Wesorick

McGraw-Hill
Children's Publishing

A Division of The McGraw-Hill Companies

Published by Instructional Fair • TS Denison
An imprint of McGraw-Hill Children's Publishing
Copyright © 2000 McGraw-Hill Children's Publishing

Send all inquiries to:
McGraw-Hill Children's Publishing
3195 Wilson Drive NW
Grand Rapids, Michigan 49544

Building Reading Comprehension—grades 1–2
ISBN: 1-56822-912-7

Table of Contents

Jan's Job

Jan loved her job. Jan juggled. First, Jan juggled jars of jam. Second, Jan juggled jars of juice. Next, Jan juggled jars of jellybeans.

Then, Jan juggled Jake the jackrabbit. But Jake the jackrabbit jerked and jumped away with the jam and the juice and the jars of jellybeans.

☞ Look at the pictures. Use 1, 2, 3, and 4 to number the pictures in the order they happened in the story.

_____   _____   _____   _____

Name _____

Rain, Rain, Go Away

Crash! Boom! It rained. Oscar painted a picture. He played with his yo-yo. He played a game with his grandpa.

Oscar waited for the rain to stop. He saw the sun. "Grandpa," he said. "Let's go outside. Let's go find it!" Oscar and his grandpa ran outside. They looked up at the sky. They looked and looked.

☞ What did Oscar and his grandpa want to find?
Circle Yes or No for each sentence.

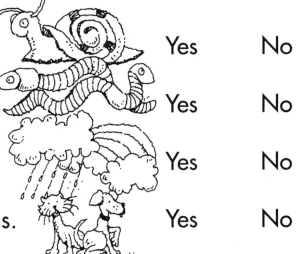

They were looking for snails.   Yes   No

They were looking for worms.   Yes   No

They were looking for a rainbow.   Yes   No

They were looking for cats and dogs.   Yes   No

Ouches in Our Pouches

What goes in our pouches?

Bees in our pouches?
No! Ouches in our pouches!

Ice skates in our pouches?
No! Ouches in our pouches!

Jacks in our pouches?
No! Ouches in our pouches!

Cactus in our pouches?
No! Ouches in our pouches!

Roses in our pouches?
No! Ouches in our pouches!

Porcupines in our pouches?
No! Ouches in our pouches!

We want soft in our pouches!
No more ouches in our pouches!

☞ Look at the squares. Write the correct words from the poem under each picture. Cut out the square that shows what the kangaroo wants in her pouch. Glue the square to the kangaroo's pouch.

Egg-stra Safe!

Humpty Dumpty
rode by a wall.
His horse tripped
and made him fall.

On his way down,
Humpty hit his head hard.
Could he be hurt?
His friends ran to the yard.

But Humpty was fine.
"I'm not hurt," Humpty said.
"I wear a hard helmet
on my egg head."

☞ Think about what happened in this rhyme. Then think about
why it happened. Draw lines to connect the cause and effect.

People hurried to see   because his horse tripped.

Humpty wasn't hurt   because Humpty hit his head.

Humpty fell   because he wore a helmet.

Name _____

Taking Care of Fifi

Ling and Juan want to make money during the summer. They have looked for a long time to find jobs. Now they have found a job they really like. Ling and Juan will take care of Fifi. Juan will take care of keeping Fifi clean and brushed. Ling will take care of feeding Fifi and giving her water.

☞ Help Ling and Juan get ready for their job. Cut out the pictures. Glue the things Ling will need in her giant bone. Glue the things Juan will need in his giant bone.

What Makes You Special?

Each person is special. Each person does something well. Read about these special children. Ziri helps animals. Josefina does her best at sports. Dana recycles. Ahmed sings. Wah is an artist.

☞ What makes each child special? Draw a line from the name to the picture.

Ziri

Josefina

Dana

Ahmed

Wah

☞ Draw a picture and write a sentence to show what makes you special. Use another sheet of paper.

Name _____

Go!

Wheelbarrow, wheelbarrow.
One wheel.
Go!

Scooter, scooter.
Two wheels.
Go!

Tricycle, tricycle.
Three wheels.
Go!

Skateboard, skateboard.
Four wheels.
Go!

Rocket ship, rocket ship.
No wheels.
Go!
Z   O   O   M!!!!

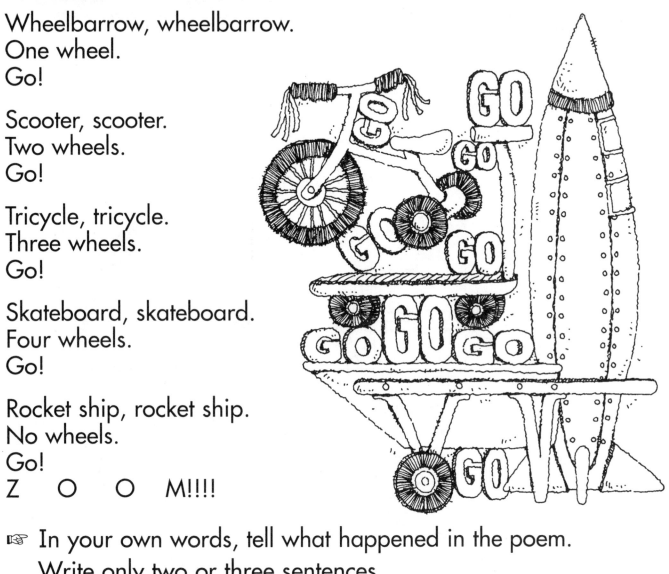

☞ In your own words, tell what happened in the poem.
    Write only two or three sentences.

_____

_____

_____

_____

_____

Name _____

And Then What Happens?

☞ Read the stories. Color the picture that shows what happens next.

Jon loves to visit his grandmother. She lives next door. He visits her every chance he gets. Jon finishes his homework early. And then what happens?

Ana starts to water the flowers. Her friend asks her to come over. They play. And then what happens?

Name _____

Li picks strawberries. He washes them well. He puts them in a bowl with pieces of banana. And then what happens?

Dina is kind and helpful. She thinks of others and what they need. Dina's brother comes home from school crying. And then what happens?

Name _____

Trunks and Necks

Elephants and giraffes are alike because they are mammals. They are different because one has a long trunk and the other has a long neck. Elephants and giraffes are both animals. But the elephant is gray, and the giraffe is yellow.

Both animals look for food when they are hungry. The elephant uses its long trunk to pick up peanuts and other food and brings it to its mouth. The giraffe can eat leaves from tall trees because it has long legs and a long neck.

Name _____

☞ Paste the boxes in the correct parts of the diagram.

an animal	long legs	long trunk
a mammal	gray	yellow
long neck	picks up peanuts	looks for food

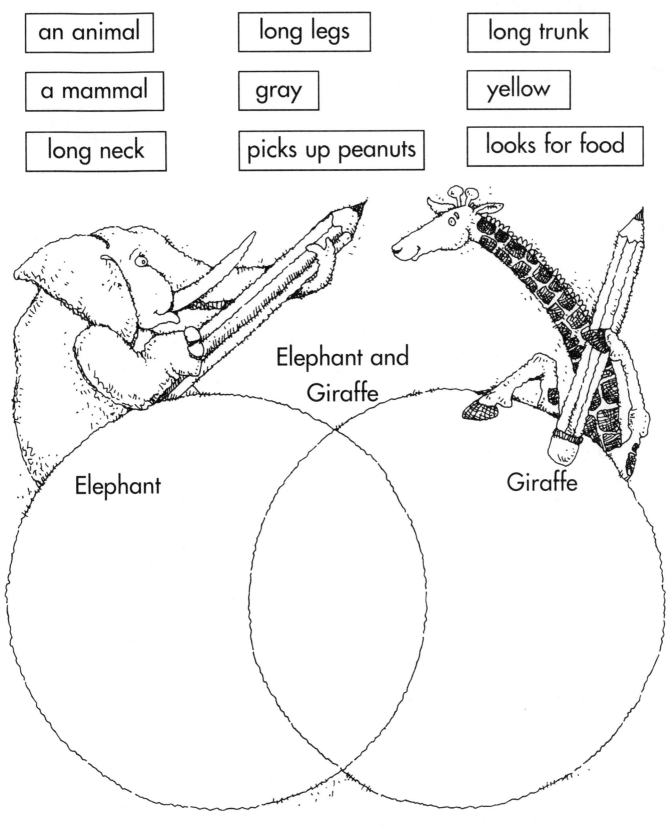

Elephant and Giraffe

Elephant

Giraffe

Name _____

Fishing for Light

What kind of fish comes out only at night? The Flashlight Fish! It has a special way to stay safe. It has lights under its eyes.

What does it do to stay safe? First, it uncovers its lights. It can do this like you can open your eyes. Next, the Flashlight Fish swims in a straight line. A dangerous fish follows the lights. Then, the Flashlight Fish covers its lights. Last, it turns and races away. The dangerous fish cannot see where the Flashlight Fish has gone. The Flashlight Fish is safe.

☞ Read the sentences. Number them in the correct order.

_____   The Flashlight Fish covers its lights.

_____   The Flashlight Fish turns and races away.

_____   The Flashlight Fish swims in a straight line.

_____   The Flashlight Fish uncovers its lights.

Rhyme Time

☞ Read each rhyme. Find the correct picture to finish each sentence. Cut it out. Glue it in the square. Write the word below the picture.

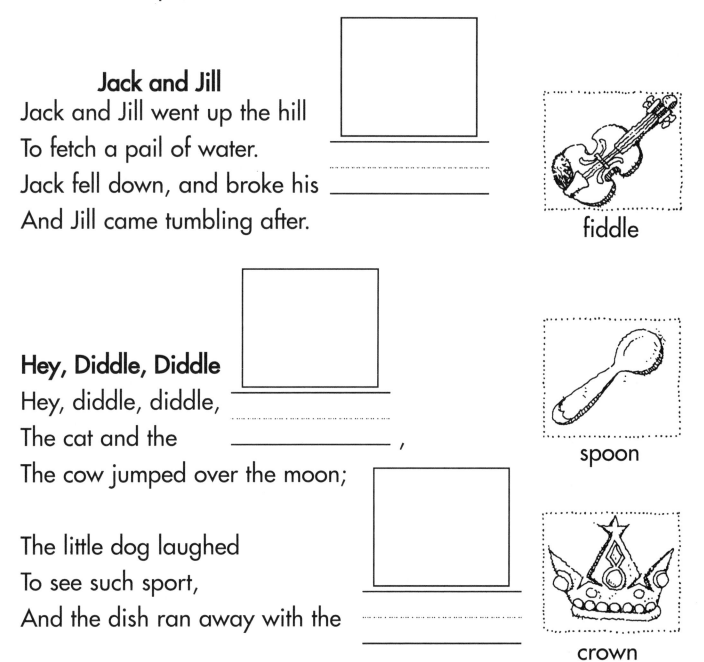

Jack and Jill
Jack and Jill went up the hill
To fetch a pail of water.
Jack fell down, and broke his _____
And Jill came tumbling after.

fiddle

Hey, Diddle, Diddle
Hey, diddle, diddle,
The cat and the _____ ,
The cow jumped over the moon;

spoon

The little dog laughed
To see such sport,
And the dish ran away with the _____

crown

Bink! Bonk!

Bonk wanted to learn to skate. Bink had been skating for a long time. Bonk asked Bink for a skating lesson. Bonk had knee pads. Bink said, "I don't need those." Bonk had a helmet. Bink said, "I don't need that."

Bonk took one step—and—boink! Bonk fell. Bink laughed. "Might as well go home," Bink told Bonk.

"I won't give up," said Bonk. Bonk fell again. But finally, Bonk took one small step and did not fall.

"Just beginner's luck," said Bink. Bink skated backward.

"Be careful," cried Bonk. "Watch where you're going."

Bink tripped on a rock. She skinned her four knees. CLONK! CLONK! CLONK! CLONK!

"I'll help you up," said Bonk. "Then maybe I can help you with another thing or four."

☞ Choose words to describe Bink and Bonk. Write the words in the ovals around their names.

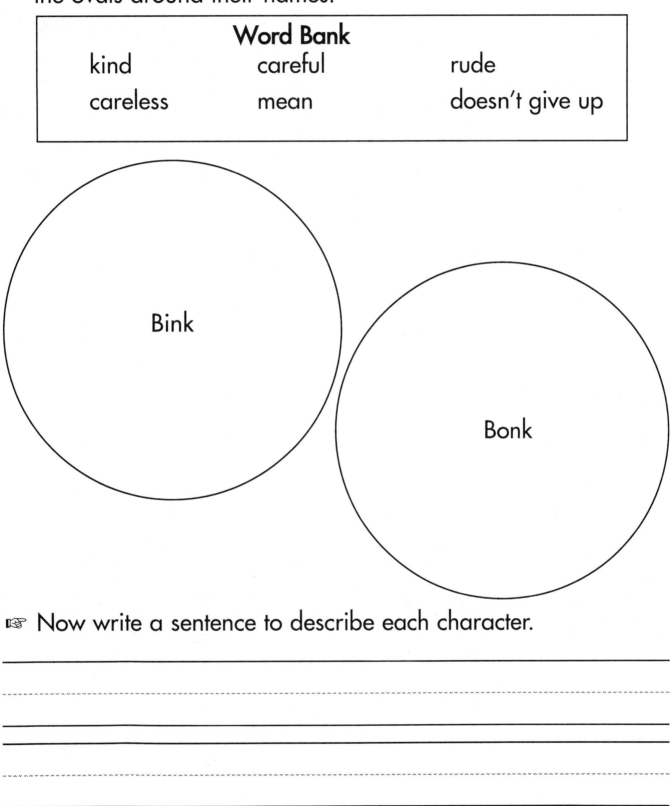

Word Bank

kind   careful   rude

careless   mean   doesn't give up

Bink

Bonk

☞ Now write a sentence to describe each character.

_____

_____

_____

Agree to Disagree

Tia had a dog. Don had a cat. Don thought cats were prettier than dogs. Tia thought dogs made better pets than cats. Tia and Don talked about the noises their pets made. Cats meow. Dogs bark. Don said dogs were louder than cats.

Don thought his cat was the best pet in the world. Tia thought her dog was the best pet in the world. Tia and Don agreed to disagree.

☞ Circle F if the sentence is a fact. Circle O if the sentence is an opinion.

F   O   1. Don thought cats were prettier than dogs.

F   O   2. Tia thought dogs made better pets than cats.

F   O   3. Cats meow.

F   O   4. Dogs bark.

F   O   5. Dogs are louder than cats.

F   O   6. Tia thought her dog was the best pet in the world.

Riddle Around

I am round. I have a net under me. I have a board behind me. Players jump near me. Players throw something orange and round through me. What am I?

1. Put a circle around the word that answers the riddle.
   fishing pole   basketball rim   lake

2. Draw a basketball over the basketball hoop.

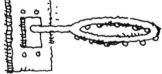

3. Draw a net under the basketball rim.

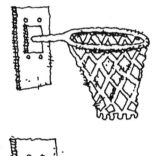

4. Draw a backboard behind the basketball hoop.

Whose Shoes?

"Happy birthday, Avi," shouted Kate. "You always have the best parties. What will we do next?"

"Let's decorate our own shoes," said Avi. He pulled five new pairs of tennis shoes from a sack.

Kate put rockets on her shoes. Avi put stripes on his. Lila drew circles all over her shoes. Mohammed glued shells on his. Resa glued stars on her shoes. Brice painted triangles on his. Avi and his friends put the shoes outside to dry.

☞ The party is over. Help Avi and his friends find their shoes.
Draw a line from the name to the correct pair.

Brice

Mohammed

Lila

Avi

Kate

Resa

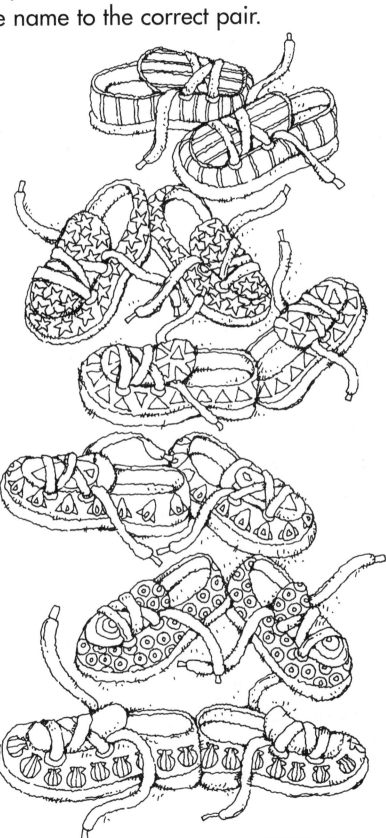

Name _____

In the Rain Forest

What do ants, parrots, monkeys, tree frogs, and snakes have in common? You can see them all in the rain forest. Some of these animals are mammals. Some are birds. Some are amphibians. Some are reptiles. These animals come in many colors. They live by eating many different things. This chart tells you about some rain forest animals.

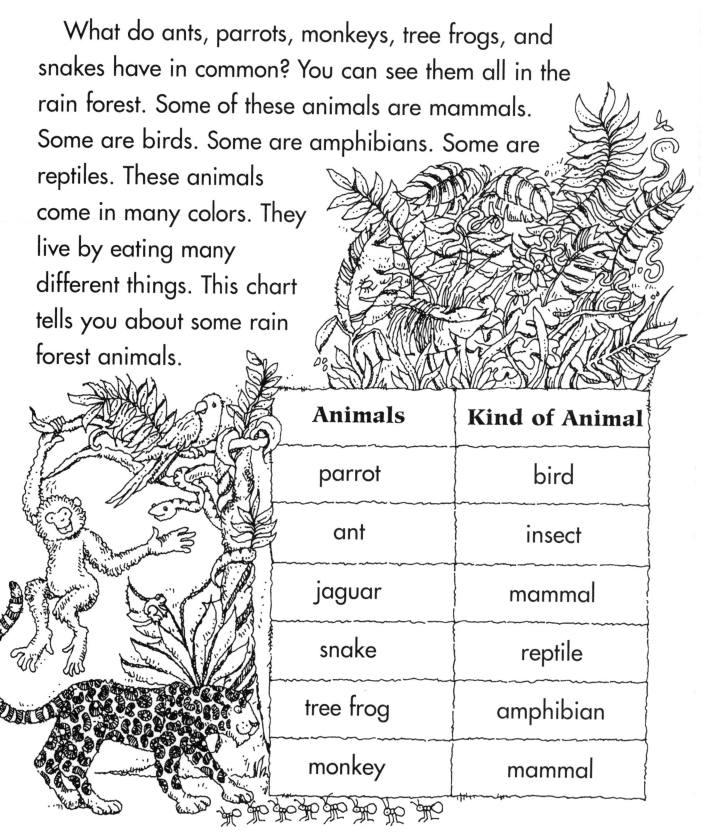

Animals	Kind of Animal
parrot	bird
ant	insect
jaguar	mammal
snake	reptile
tree frog	amphibian
monkey	mammal

Name _____

☞ Circle the picture that answers each question.

1. Which animal is an amphibian?
   (tree frog or monkey)

2. Which animals are both mammals?
   (ant and jaguar or jaguar and monkey)

3. Which animal is a reptile?
   (snake or ant)

4. Which animal is an insect?
   (tree frog or ant)

Name _____

Reduce, Reuse, Recycle

"I have a great idea," said Dax. "Let's put all the garbage in the world in a submarine. We could send it to the bottom of the ocean."

"That would cost too much money," said Marie. "And it would pollute the ocean. Pretty soon, the garbage would be floating in the water."

"How about sending all the garbage to space?" Dax asked.

"That would pollute space! And it would be too much money. I think we can help here on earth," Maria added. "In my family, we recycle. We put plastic in one bin. We put paper in another bin. Glass and cans go in their own bins. Then our garbage is remade into new products."

Name _____

☞ Help Dax and Marie recycle. Cut out the pictures. Glue them in the correct bins.

Name _____

Go Anywhere!

"I'd love to go sailing and see dolphins in the ocean," Lon told his friends. "If you could go anywhere, where would it be?"

"I want to go to the moon," said Diana.

"I want to go to South America," cried Troon.

"I wish I could go on safari in Africa," sighed Ralph.

"I wish I could go to Alaska," said Troon's grandfather.

"I know how we can all go where we want to. And we can do it in one place," Lon said. "Here are the clues. I'll meet you there." Lon gave the clues to his friends. He left.

Lon's Clues
1. Leave school and go south on First Street.
2. Turn east on A Street.
3. Walk down A Street past the shoe store.
4. Turn south on Second Street.
5. Go past the park and stop when you see the flag.

☞ Follow Lon's clues on the map below. Draw a line to show Lon's friends the way.

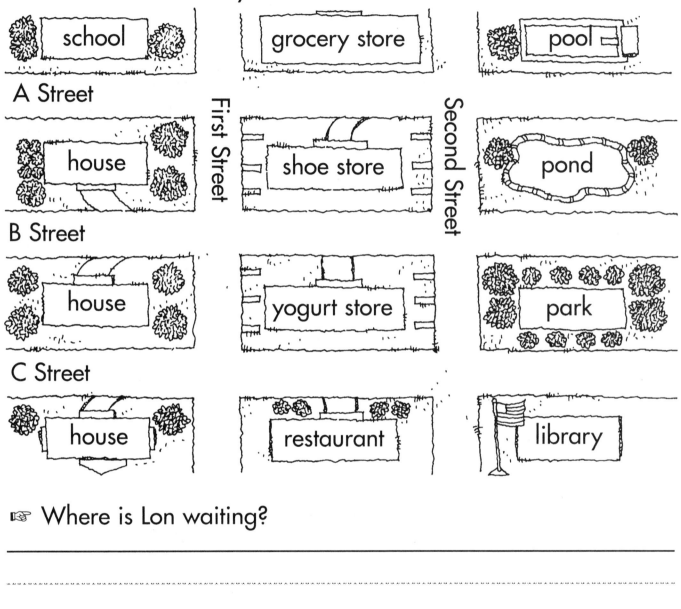

☞ Where is Lon waiting?

_____

- -

_____

☞ How can people go to many places there?

_____

- -

_____

_____

- -

Name _____

Flying the Friendly Skies

Airplanes have not always looked like they do today. The first planes had room for only one person, the pilot. Nothing covered the pilot's seat. Dirt blew into the pilot's face. There were no seat belts. Sometimes, pilots fell out of their planes! Airplanes have come a long way.

☞ Use the chart to show how airplanes have changed.

First Planes	Planes Today

☞ How do you think planes will look when you grow up? Draw a picture.

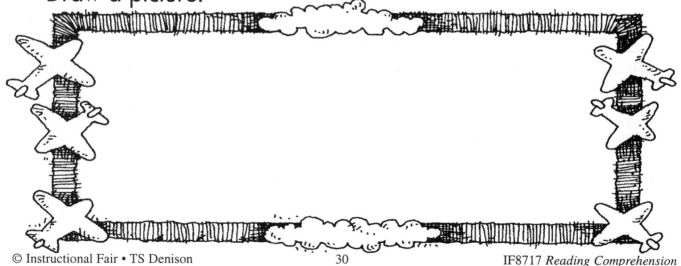

It's a Fact! Or Is It?

Nelly Bly wanted to work for a newspaper in 1885. Many people thought women could not do this job. Nelly Bly asked a man for a newspaper job. The man thought women should not have jobs. But Nelly Bly proved she could write. She got the job. She wrote many news stories.

☞ Read the sentences. Write the letter F in the newspaper if the sentence states a fact. Write the letter O if the sentence states an opinion.

1. Nelly Bly asked for a newspaper job.

2. Women cannot do this job.

3. Women should not have jobs.

4. Nelly got the job.

☞ Write one fact and one opinion about a family member.

Name _____

Team Work

Animals can work in teams. Some small fish eat food from the teeth of big fish. Then the big fish gets clean teeth!

Sometimes animals help each other stay safe. One animal can do a good job of seeing. The other animal can do a good job of hearing. The animals stay close. One animal listens. The other animal watches.

Ants can get food from some small bugs. Then the ants keep the small bugs safe from bigger bugs.

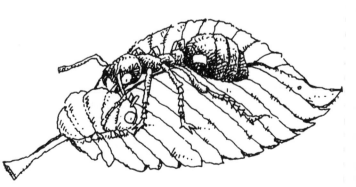

Animal teams can work well together.

Name _____

☞ Circle the correct answer. Then draw your own animal team.

1. This story is mostly about _____.

    bugs   ants   animal teams

2. Sometimes small fish clean the teeth of _____.

    ants   big fish   bugs

3. Ants help keep small bugs safe from _____.

    big bugs   big fish   little fish

4. Animals can help each other stay _____.

    afraid   safe   bug

Tornado!

The dark sky made it look like midnight at noon. We looked out the windows. A tornado raced toward our house. We dashed away from the windows. We ran into the bathroom and closed the door. We jumped into the bathtub. I heard a loud roar like a train. "Cover your heads," I yelled.

1. The people in the story saw a tornado. Why did they run away from the windows?

_____

_____

_____

_____

2. Why did the people in the story go into the bathroom and get into the bathtub?

_____

_____

_____

_____

Under the Sea

☞ Everyone is getting ready for the big play "Under the Sea." Dolphin Director is giving stage directions. Read her directions. Then draw the animals in their places.

"Take your places. Glub, glub," says Dolphin Director.

", put on a purple . Swim over to the table. you'll be the queen. Put on a gold . Walk to the top of the . , tie a red around your tail. Bob over to the mirror. wrap around the next to the to give us light."

Robbie's Job

Robbie is very smart. She loves to read. She likes to argue. She gives many good reasons when she argues.

Robbie likes to help people. Once, one of her friends bought a yo-yo at a store. The yo-yo broke the first time her friend tried to play with it. Robbie went to the store with her friend. Robbie talked to the manager. The manager took back the yo-yo and gave Robbie's friend a new one.

Robbie often thinks about what she would like to do when she gets older.

☞ What jobs does Robbie think about? Unscramble the letters to find out. Write each job name.

1. Robbie thinks about being a _____ and helping sick people in a hospital.   cootdr

2. Robbie thinks about being a _____ and working with students in a classroom.   chetrae

3. Robbie thinks about being a _____ and going to court to talk to a judge.   lyrewa

4. Robbie thinks about being a _____ and helping sick animals.   tve

☞ Which job do you think would be best for Robbie? Why?

_____

_____

_____

_____

Way to Grow!

Sean plants a vegetable garden. He plants his vegetables where they will get sunshine. He waters his vegetables. He feeds them plant food.

Rob plants a vegetable garden, too. He plants his vegetables in a place with very little sunshine. He doesn't water his vegetables. He doesn't feed them plant food.

☞ Draw what the vegetable gardens will look like this summer. Write the boys' names above their gardens.

 _____

 _____

☞ What would you like to plant in a garden?
Draw a picture of your garden.

Name _____

I Can!

Sue stamped her little leg. "I can't do anything right!" she buzzed. She watched her honeycomb crumble. Sue sat down in the soft honey and put her head in her hands.

Just then, Sue heard her friend Rusty bark. He was hurt. Sue zoomed down and saw a thorn stuck in Rusty's paw. At first, she was afraid to help her friend. "I won't do it right," she buzzed. Her little heart raced.

But then Sue had a plan. She put honey on a leaf. She stuck the leaf to the thorn. She pulled it out! Rusty wagged his tail.

☞ Circle the correct answer.

1. Sue is a

2. Sue's friend is a

3. Sue is . . .   mean   kind   rude.

4. At the end of the story, the friend is...   sad   scared   happy.

☞ Draw a picture of Sue and her friend.

39

Name _____

Moon Walk

What is it like to walk on the moon? Astronauts Neil Armstrong and Buzz Aldrin walked on the moon. They took pictures. People on earth saw the pictures on television. The astronauts gathered rocks and dirt on the moon. Then they came back to Earth in Apollo 11. Apollo 11 splashed into the ocean. The astronauts were heroes.

☞ Circle Yes or No for each sentence.

1. Neil Armstrong watched television on the moon.   Yes   No

2. Buzz Aldrin walked on the moon.   Yes   No

3. The astronauts gathered rocks on the moon.   Yes   No

4. People took pictures of them on the moon.   Yes   No

5. Apollo 11 splashed into the ocean.   Yes   No

☞ Draw a picture of yourself walking on the moon.

Pet Match

Jamila has a job. She gives baths to her friends' pets. Her friends are coming to pick up the pets. Help Jamila match the pets to their owners.

☞ Read the clues. Cut out the pets.
    Glue each pet below its owner's name.

1. Kenya's pet is a dog.
2. The cat belongs to the girl near flowers.
3. A pig is between the dog and the cat.
4. A hamster is between the dog and a horse.

Jeremy	Adrian	Kenya	Bob	Ashley

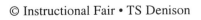

Clowning Around

Zane blows out his candles. A clown tumbles in through the door. She blows up balloons. She twists them and turns them to make dogs. Then she stands on her head and plays a song on the harmonica. Smoke appears, and the clown disappears. This is Zane's best birthday party ever!

☞ Cut out the pictures on page 43. Glue them in the correct order.

Name _____

Yum! Yum!

☞ It's picnic time! Everyone in the class is making something special. Read the sentences. Then circle the picture that shows what each family will take to the picnic.

Sam gathers lemons. His uncle cuts them. Sam squeezes the juice into a pitcher. He adds sugar and water. Sam puts in lemon slices and ice. He stirs. Sam and his uncle are making . . .

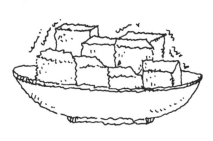

Ana-Maria and her dad put flour, sugar, water, and an egg into a bowl. Ana-Maria adds melted chocolate. They stir the mixture. Then she puts the mixture in a pan. Ana-Maria's dad puts the pan in the oven. Frosting will come later. Ana-Maria and her dad are making . . .

Name _____

Ali and his mom buy a roll of dough at the grocery store. His mom cuts the dough into circles. Ali puts them on a long metal sheet. His mom puts them in the oven. Ali and his mom are making . . .

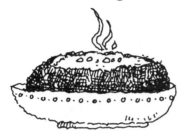 

Cela gets lettuce, tomatoes, and cucumbers from her garden. Her grandfather cuts them into pieces. Cela puts the pieces into a bowl. Cela and her grandfather are making . . .

☞ Draw a picture of your favorite food to take to a picnic.

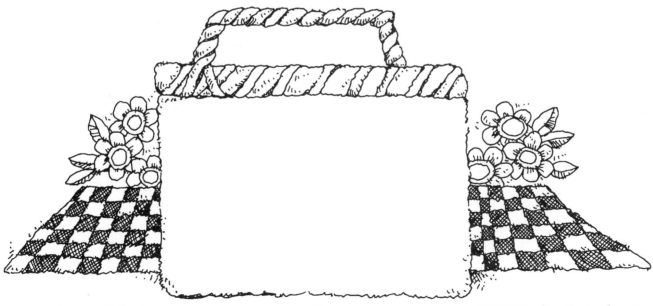

Name _____

Hats Off!

Kamal collects hats. He saves his hats in boxes. Kamal's aunt came to visit. Kamal took his hats out of their boxes. He wanted to show them to his aunt. He sorted his hats. He lined them up.

☞ Read about Kamal's hats.

1. Kamal has two big western hats.

2. Kamal has three baseball hats.

3. Kamal has one clown hat.

4. Kamal has two chef hats.

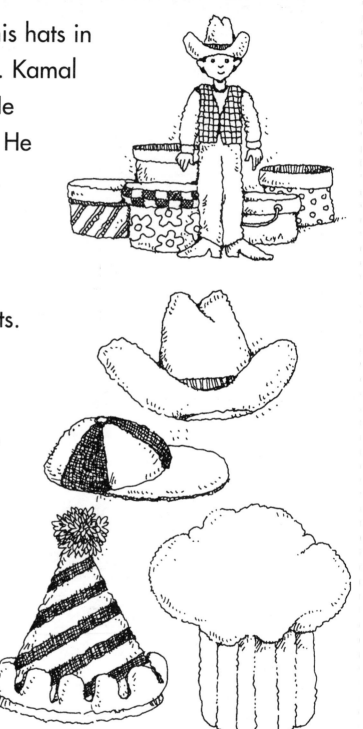

☞ Cut out the hats at the bottom of the page. Put each hat in the correct place on the chart.

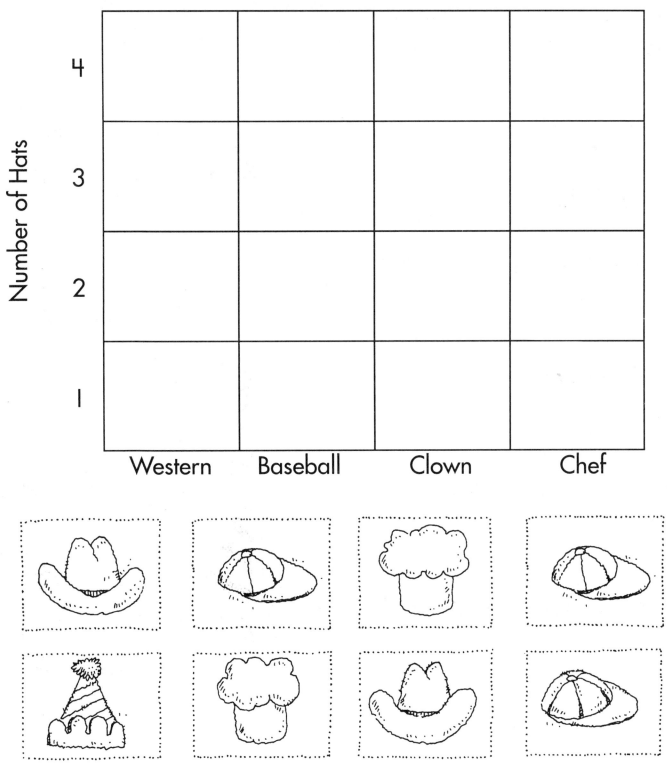

Kamal's Hats

Name _____

A Horse of a Different Color

"I can't wait for our turn," said Noreen.

"I know," replied Fred. "It's been a long time since we rode horses."

"Is it time yet?" asked Kwan.

"Yes," said Anna. She turned to Will. "Are you ready?"

"I'm not sure," said Will.

At the stable door, Will couldn't believe what he saw. All the horses had turned bright colors. "I don't feel so scared anymore," he said. He dashed to the blue horse.

"I want the green horse," cried Noreen.

"Red for Fred," said Fred.

Anna ran to the orange horse.

"The purple one is mine," said Kwan.

Name _____

☞ Color each horse the correct color.

Name _____

It's Cold Outside!

"Let's go play outside," said Jada to her grandma.

"It sure is cold," said Grandma. "Do you have your mittens?"

"Yes," said Jada. She and Grandma stepped outside.

Jada and Grandma played in the tall white drifts. They made big white balls and threw them. Little flakes began to fall. "Looks like we'll get a few more inches today," Jada said.

Name _____

☞ What happened before Jada and her grandma went outside? Circle Yes or No for each sentence.

1. The hot sun shone for many hours.   Yes   No

2. Jada played outside in her shorts.   Yes   No

3. Snow fell for many hours.   Yes   No

4. Jada swam outside in the swimming pool.   Yes   No

☞ Draw a picture of Jada and her grandma playing outside.

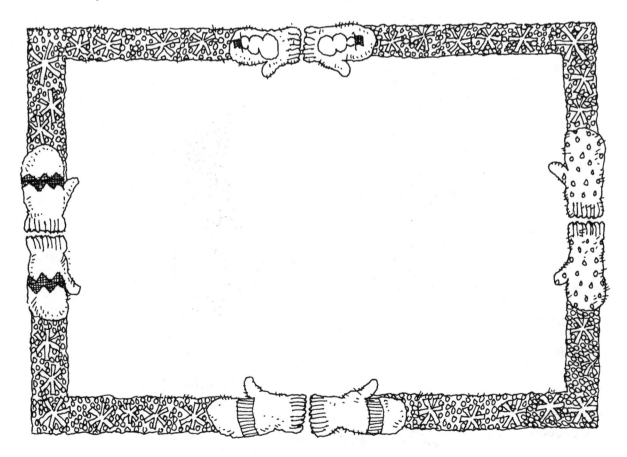

Could This Really Happen?

☞ Read each story. Decide whether each could really happen. Circle the correct answer.

Zena hurried. She didn't want to be late for her baseball game. All of a sudden, wings grew on her back. She flew all the way to the field.

‣ This could really happen.
‣ This could not really happen.

The hot summer sun dried out the garden. Alex wanted his flowers to grow. He got the hose and watered his flowers.

‣ This could really happen.
‣ This could not really happen.

Name _____

David saved money all month. He wanted to buy a special gift for his grandfather. He bought a book about painting. He knew his grandfather would love it.

▸ This could really happen.
▸ This could not really happen.

Michelle learned about the stars. She learned about Planet Mars. Michelle pulled stars from the sky. She made stairs from the stars. She walked all the way up her starry staircase to Mars.

▸ This could really happen.
▸ This could not really happen.

Name _____

Long Ago

Dinosaurs lived long ago. All dinosaurs were reptiles, like lizards. But not all dinosaurs were large. Some were as small as chickens. Some dinosaurs ate other animals. Many dinosaurs ate only plants. No people lived when dinosaurs were alive.

☞ Write the correct word in each blank.

Word Bank	No	Some	Many	All

1. _____ dinosaurs ate meat.

2. _____ dinosaurs were reptiles.

3. _____ people lived when dinosaurs were alive.

4. _____ dinosaurs ate only plants.

☞ Draw your own dinosaur picture.

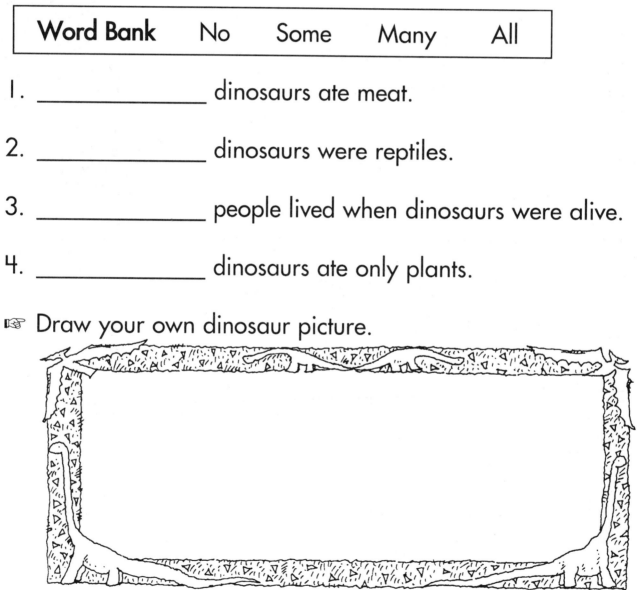

Talk to the Animals

Can a gorilla talk? Gorillas don't form words the way humans do. But they can make known what they want to say. One gorilla, Koko, learned sign language. She talked with her hands. And she understood words humans said.

Dr. Penny Patterson is the scientist who taught sign language to Koko. She showed Koko a picture of the two of them together. Penny pointed to Koko in the picture and asked, "Who's that?"

Koko answered by signing her own name, Koko.

☞ In your own words, write what happened in the story above.

_____

···

_____

_____

···

_____

_____

···

_____

Name _____

Who's Afraid?

"We're going to the beach for my birthday!" said Sandra. "Can you come?"

"I don't know," said her friend Kim. "I'm afraid of the water."

"Please come," said Sandra. "You don't have to get in the water. Just come and have some birthday cake." Kim agreed.

At the beach, Kim played in the sand. She built sand castles. She threw beach balls. She wrote her name in the sand with a stick.

As Kim picked up a beach ball, she heard a shout. "Help," yelled Sandra. "I hurt my toe on a rock. I can't walk back."

"The water scares me," cried Kim.

"Please," yelled Sandra. "I need you."

Kim dashed toward Sandra. She got to the edge of the water. Her heart raced. I don't know if I can do it, she thought. She looked at her friend. Sandra needs me, she thought. Kim walked bravely into the water. She helped Sandra out of the water.

"Thank you," said Sandra. "You're a true friend."

Name _____

☞ **In the beach balls, write what happens at the beginning, middle, and end of the story.**

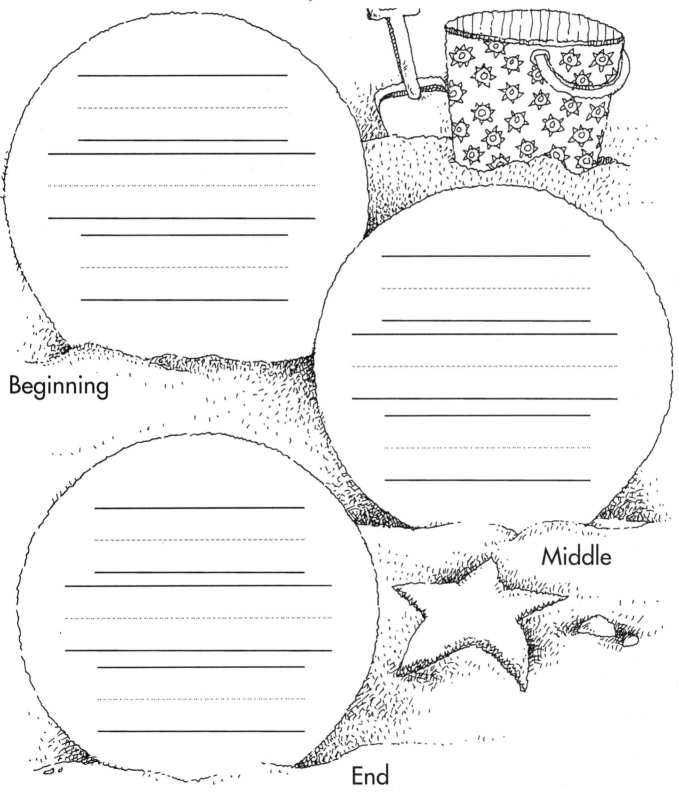

Beginning

Middle

End

Where and When?

☞ Every story happens at a place and time. Read each story. Cut out each square at the bottom of the next page. Glue it next to the story it matches.

The clock showed midnight. Two mice friends sat in their home. They talked about the things they wanted to do. One wanted to eat all the cheese in the world. The other wanted to break all the mice traps in the world.

Juan and Don went to school early in the morning. They sat at their desks. The teacher read a book about dolphins. Then Juan and Don wrote books of their own.

Name _____

The year is 3010. Rae and Raphael zoom into space. Their spaceship moves faster than the speed of light. They race toward the moon.

Up, Up, and Away

☞ Choose the correct word from the balloon for each line. Write the correct word on the line.

Word Bank

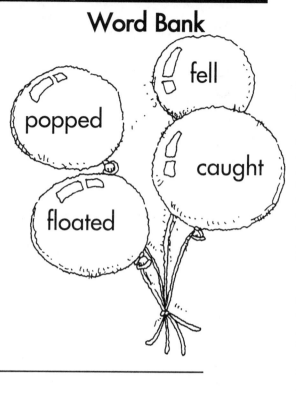

Tan and Sam went to the zoo.

Whoops! Tan <u>let go of her balloon.</u>

Tan's balloon .... up

_____

into the sky. Sam shared his balloon

with Tan. Tan said, "Thank you."

Sam dropped his ice cream cone. It ....

_____

down to the ground. What a mess!

Tan's grandpa held his balloon too close to the point on a

fence. His balloon ....

_____

Sam's brother <u>had a long string</u> on his balloon. The string

got .... in a tree. Sam's brother couldn't get it

_____

loose. He had to get another balloon.

Name _____

Paul's Pasta

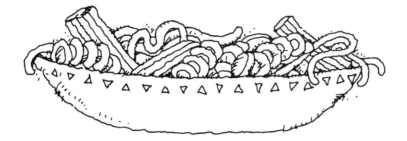

Paul wanted to make pasta salad. First, he put cooked pasta in a bowl. Second, he put yogurt in the bowl. Next, he added celery. Then, he added tomatoes. Last, he stirred.

☞ Read the sentences. Number them in the correct order.

He added celery.

He stirred.

He put cooked pasta in a bowl.

He added tomatoes.

He put yogurt in the bowl.

Ocean View

When you think of fish, do you think of fliers and rats? Flying fish and rat-tail fish both live in the ocean. Flying fish live near the top of the ocean. Rat-tail fish do not live near the top of the ocean. They live deeper.

Flying fish can swim. Rat-tail fish can swim, too. Flying fish can jump a long way across the top of the water. Rat-tail fish cannot. Rat-tail fish have long tails. But flying fish do not have long tails.

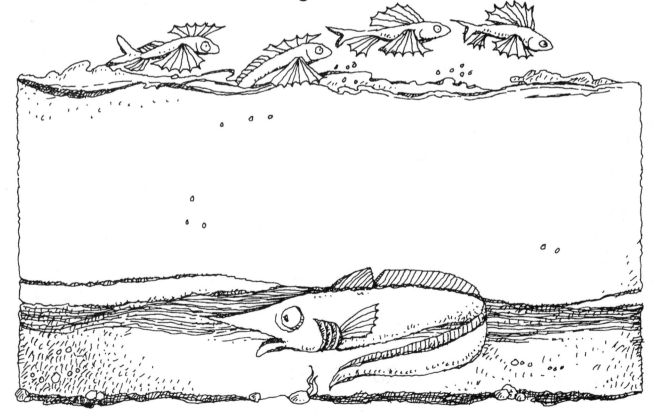

☞ Tell how flying fish and rat-tail fish are alike and different by writing about them in the diagram.

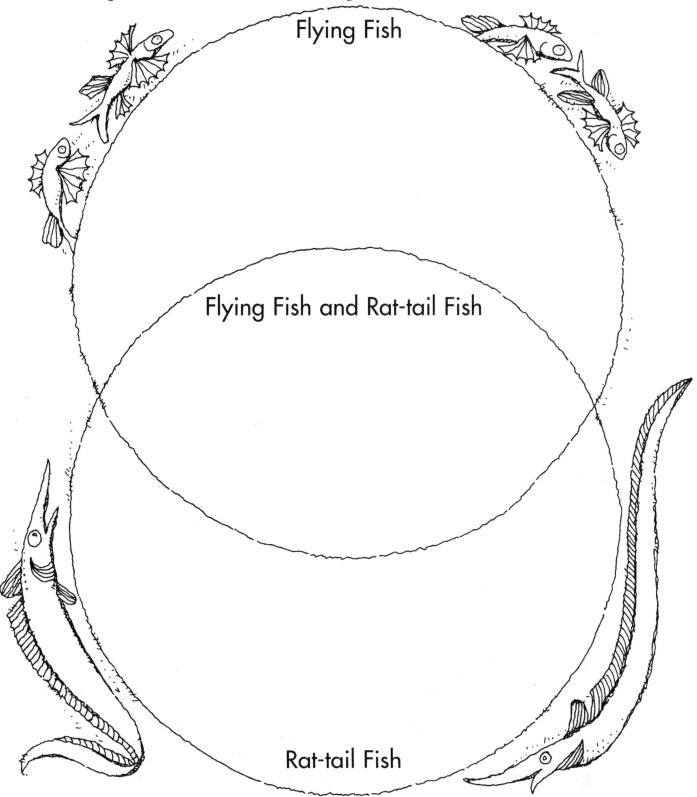

Flying Fish

Flying Fish and Rat-tail Fish

Rat-tail Fish

Name _____

Planets and Moons

How many moons do you see when you look up into the sky at night? You only see one, of course. The Earth has only one moon. Did you know that other planets have more than one moon? And some have none at all.

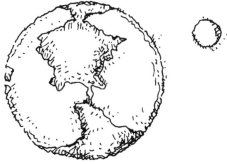

☞ Look at the chart to find how many moons each planet has.

Planets	Number of Moons
Mercury	0
Venus	0
Earth	1
Mars	2
Jupiter	16
Pluto	1

64

Name _____

☞ Circle the correct answer to each question.

1. Which planet has two moons?

   Venus   Mars

2. Which planets have no moons?

   Venus and Pluto   Mercury and Venus

3. Which planet has the same number of moons as Earth?

   Mars   Pluto

4. Which planet on the chart has the greatest
   number of moons?

   Jupiter   Venus

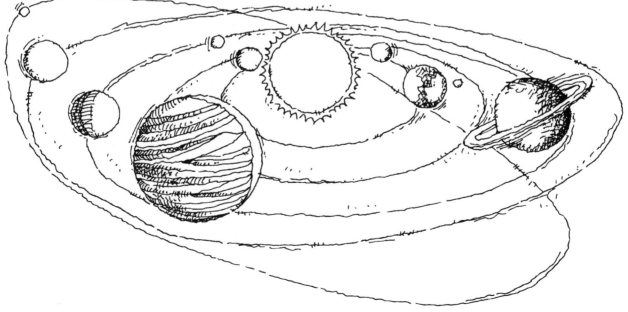

Could This Be Real?

☞ Read the sentences. Could the action in each sentence really happen? Circle Yes or No for each sentence.

1. Sasha rode his 　　　　　　high in the sky.

　　Yes　　　　No

2. Tanya went to the 　　　　　　for a check-up.

　　Yes　　　　No

3. Anya and Rob played

　　Yes　　　　No

4. Suki rode all the way across the top of a on her bicycle.

　　Yes　　　　No

5. Sabine and her aunt took their 　　　　for a walk around the block.

　　Yes　　　　No

Name _____

☞ Draw two pictures. In one square, show something that could really happen. In the other square, show something that could not really happen.

Could Really Happen

Could Not Really Happen

Picnic Poster

"I can't believe the school picnic is next week," said Casey.

"Neither can I," said Tad. "That means summer is just around the corner. Do you want to make posters to tell everyone about the picnic?"

"Sure," said Tad. "What should the posters say?"

"They should let people know that the picnic will be on Sunday. That's May 25th. And it will be at Silas Park. Everyone should bring food. Be sure to sign your posters so everyone will know that you made them."

☞ Help Tad finish the poster for the picnic.

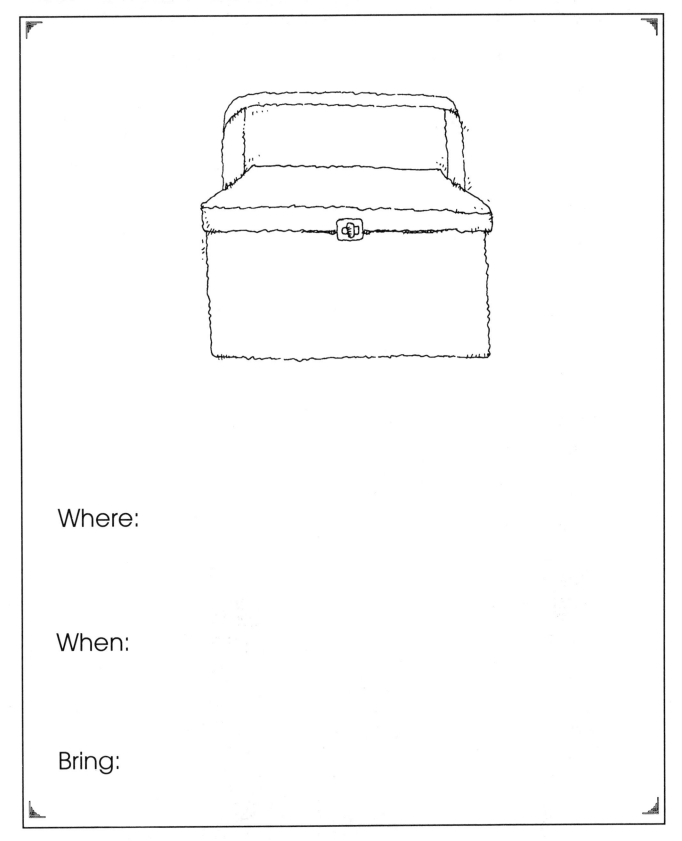

Where:

When:

Bring:

Ring Around the Moon

Sadie Space Officer flew on her nightly patrol. "How are you, Pluto?" she asked.

"Fine," answered Pluto.

"Having a good night?" she asked Venus.

"The best." Venus glowed.

When Sadie flew close to Mars, she worried. Mars frowned. Tears rolled down Mars' craters and made huge pools. "What's the matter, Mars?" she asked. "How can I help?"

"One of my moons got a ring for a gift. But the ring is lost. My moon is so sad. Now it doesn't give any moonlight. My poor moon!" Mars sniffled.

"I have an idea!" cried Sadie Space Officer. She raced off toward Saturn. She flew back carrying a sparkling ring. "Will this help?" she asked.

Mars smiled a smile that crossed all Mars' craters. Sadie tossed the ring to Mars' moon. Instantly, the moon grew bright.

"All is well with my planets," said Sadie.

Name _____

☞ Cut out the pictures from the bottom of the page. Glue them in the correct order.

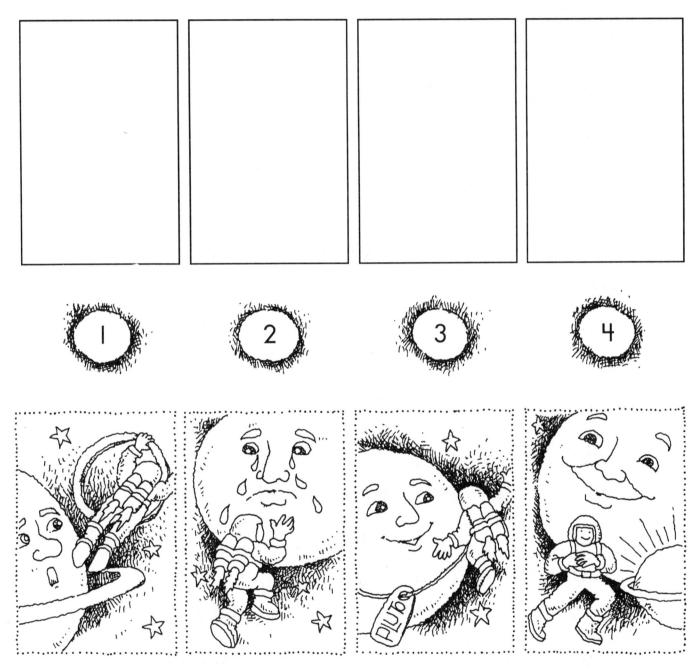

Too Big

Barker wished she was the biggest dog on the block. Every time Barker saw Bruiser, she hung her head. I'll never be that big, she thought. What good is a little dog? A big dog can carry newspapers. She can chase away pesky cats. She can do it all. And I can't do anything.

One day, Barker padded along the sidewalk. "Help," someone cried. Barker ran to check out the problem. Bruiser stood nearby.

"A boy is caught in the bushes on the other side of the wall," Bruiser said. "There's a small hole, but I can't get through."

Barker trotted through the hole. She tugged on the branches wrapped around the child's ankle. She got the boy free. "Thank you," cried the boy. The boy hugged Barker and patted her head.

Barker licked the boy's face. Barker saw Bruiser looking through the hole. Bruiser said, "Good job, Barker." Barker wagged her tail.

Name _____

☞ **Think about how Barker changes in this story.**

1. Circle the paw that shows how Barker feels at the beginning of the story.

2. Write a word that tells how Barker feels at the beginning of the story.

_____

_____

3. Circle the paw that shows how Barker feels at the end of the story.

4. Write a word that tells how Barker feels at the end of the story.

_____

_____

5. Why do Barker's feelings change at the end of the story?

_____

_____

_____

_____

Name _____

Time to Camp

Camping can be fun. But it's important to prepare for a camping trip. You'll need food and drinks. Bring marshmallows for a tasty treat. Be sure to take warm clothes for cool evenings. Your shoes should feel good on your feet. You'll need a flashlight. Take a backpack that's not too heavy if you plan to hike. Don't forget your tent! Be sure it's set well into the ground. You don't want it to blow over in a strong wind!

☞ These tents blew over in the wind. Unscramble the letters in each little tent. Write the words in the sentences.

Bring marshmallows for a _____ treat.

tstay

You'll need a _____.

hthgllfais

It's important to prepare for a _____ trip.

gciampn

Your shoes should _____ good on your feet.

efel

☞ Carefully cut out the sentences on the bottom of page 74. Glue the main idea sentence above the tent. Glue the supporting sentences inside the tent.

Main Idea

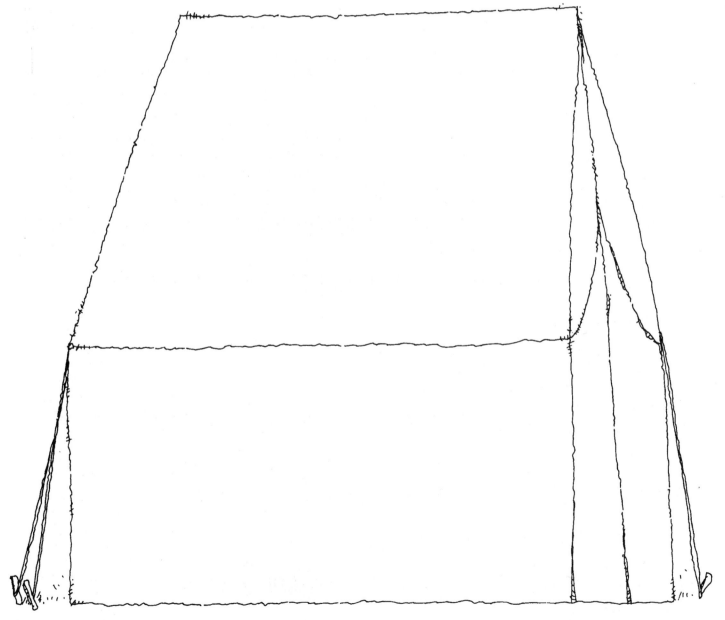

Elephant Gardens

Eli Elephant has two gardens. He has a flower garden and a vegetable garden. Eli waters his gardens with his trunk. Follow the directions to give Eli's gardens more color.

1. Color the pond blue.

2. Color Eli gray.

3. Use a pencil to draw water coming from Eli's trunk to water the gardens.

4. Color the short flowers purple.

5. Color the tall flowers orange.

6. Draw a green circle around the vegetable garden.

Name _____

Guiding the Way

Tessa is not able to see. But she has a guide dog to help her. Her guide dog, Delia, helps in many ways. Delia guides Tessa to school. Delia is very careful as she and Tessa cross the street. Tessa can tell Delia to go straight, to turn, or to stop. Delia listens carefully.

Tessa gives Delia big hugs. Delia snuggles with Tessa and gives her big kisses.

☞ Choose four words that tell about the guide dog Delia. Write the words in the boxes.

Word Bank

mean   kind   helpful
loving   angry   selfish   careful

☞ Tell why a dog like Delia is important to Tessa.

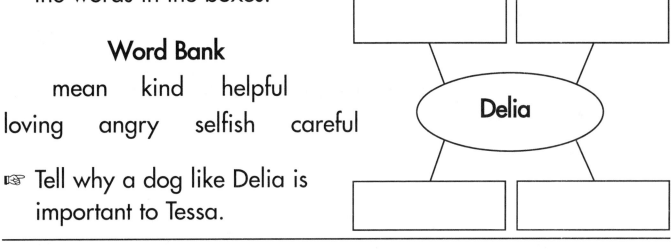

Delia

_____

_____

_____

_____

Name _____

The Earth Is a Puzzle

Have you ever thought of the earth's surface as a puzzle? The outer shell of the earth is called the crust. The crust is made up of plates—not the kind you put your food on. These plates come together like the pieces of a puzzle. Mountains can spring up when plates smash together. Earthquakes can occur when plates slide past each other.

land

crust

ocean

☞ In your own words, tell about how the earth is a puzzle. Write 2 or 3 sentences.

_____

_____

_____

_____

_____

_____

Name _____

☞ Cut out the earth puzzle pieces below. Glue them inside the
circle to make a model of the earth.

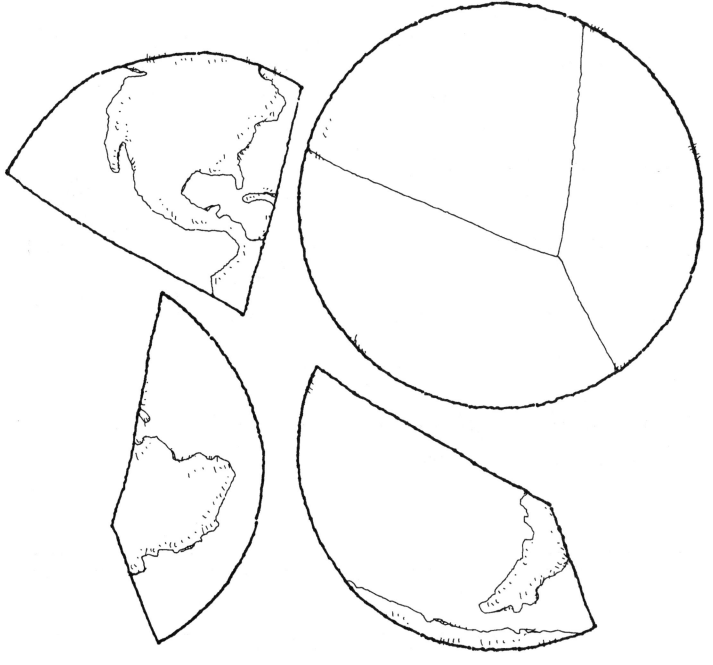

Through the Hoop

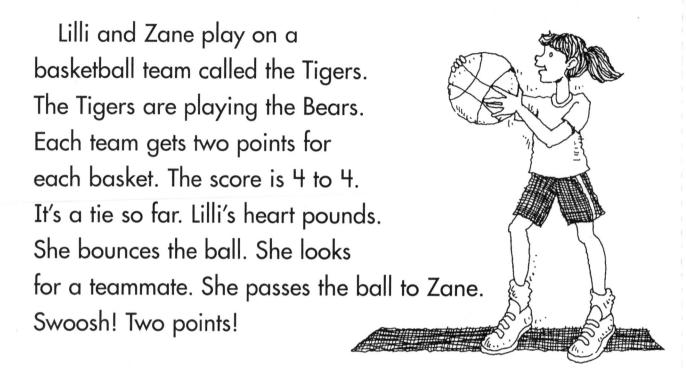

Lilli and Zane play on a basketball team called the Tigers. The Tigers are playing the Bears. Each team gets two points for each basket. The score is 4 to 4. It's a tie so far. Lilli's heart pounds. She bounces the ball. She looks for a teammate. She passes the ball to Zane. Swoosh! Two points!

A member of the Bears team grabs the ball. She races to the other end of the court. She makes a basket.

Lilli jumps into action. She bounces the ball all the way back to her basket. She sinks the ball through the basket. One of the Bears scoops up the ball, runs across the court, and makes another basket. The game is over.

☞ Who wins the game? Make your own scoreboard to show who wins. Write a 2 for every basket each team makes.

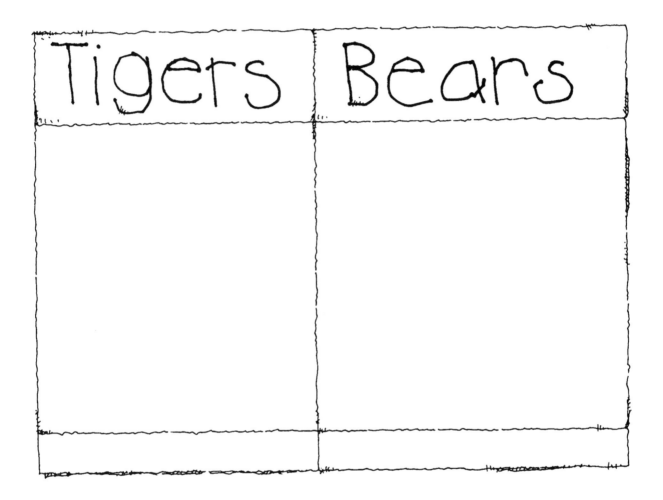

☞ Circle the correct answer.

1. The Tigers won.   Yes   No

2. The Bears won.   Yes   No

3. The game ended in a tie.   Yes   No

Name _____

Building Up

Kiki's class is building a block city. They have colored blocks. The blocks are green, orange, and red. Group A is building a store. Group B is making a bank. Group C is building a library. Group D is working on a school.

☞ Read the chart to find out which blocks each group is using.

	Green blocks	Orange blocks	Red blocks
Group A	5	3	0
Group B	6	7	1
Group C	0	4	5
Group D	1	2	7

Name _____

☞ Read the chart on page 82 and answer the questions below.

1. Which group is using the most red blocks?

_____

_____

2. Which group is using no red blocks?

_____

_____

3. Which group is using the fewest orange blocks?

_____

_____

4. Which group is using the most blocks altogether?

_____

_____

5. Which group is using the fewest blocks altogether?

_____

_____

What Would You Expect?

☞ Read each story. Circle the answer to tell what will happen next.

Isabel threw a little rock into a pond. Circles rippled out in the water around the little rock. More and more circles rippled until the ripples reached the shore.

1. What will happen if Isabel throws another little rock into the pond?

    All the water in the pond will splash out.

    Circles will ripple out into the water.

Terry never ate anything sweet. He went to Gina's party. Gina served sandwiches, popcorn, ice cream, and birthday cake. Terry had fun.

2. What did Terry eat?

    cake and popcorn

    sandwiches and popcorn

    ice cream and sandwiches

Name _____

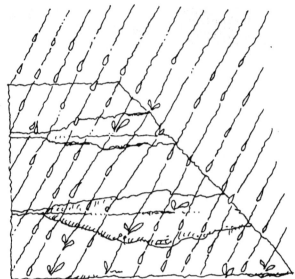

The rain went on for hours and hours. Puddles formed in the streets. But the sun finally came out. The temperature rose to more than 100 degrees. The temperature stayed that hot for two days. There was no more rain.

3. What happened after those two days?

The puddles were gone.

The puddles were bigger.

The puddles were the same size.

Chin loves to count. She counts everything. She counts leaves. She even counts clouds. The math test is tomorrow. Chin practices counting and adding all evening.

4. How will Chin do on the test?

Chin will do poorly.

Chin will not take the test.

Chin will do well.

Name _____

Earthquake!

All earthquakes cause shaking. Some earthquakes cause problems. Most earthquakes in the United States happen near the Pacific Ocean. Many buildings there are built in a special way. This helps keep people safe during an earthquake. No earthquakes happen in outer space.

FAULT LINE

PACIFIC OCEAN

☞ Write the words at the bottom of the page in the correct sentences.

1. _____ buildings near the Pacific Ocean are built in a special way.

2. _____ earthquakes cause shaking.

3. _____ earthquakes happen in outer space.

4. _____ earthquakes cause problems.

5. _____ earthquakes in the United States happen near the Pacific Ocean.

Some   **All**   **Most**   **Many**   **No**

Up in the Sky, Down on the Ground

What do you think of when you think of a bird? Do you think of an animal spreading its wings? Do you think of it flying through the sky? Would you be surprised to find out that some birds can't fly at all?

Kiwi birds can't fly. Their wings are very tiny and will not hold them up. Ostriches can't fly. Like kiwis, their wings are not strong enough to help them fly. Penguins cannot fly. Their small wings are more like swimming flippers. Their wings help them swim.

☞ Choose the correct answer. Write it on the line.

1. This story is mostly about _____.

     kiwis   ostriches   birds that can't fly

2. The kiwi's wings are _____.

     big   small   strong

3. A penguin's wings are _____.

     big   like flippers   strong

Name _____

Pollution Solution

Air pollution causes many problems. It makes air unsafe to breathe. Smoke causes air pollution. Smoke can put dangerous chemicals in the air. Cars cause air pollution. Cutting down too many trees is bad for the air.

What can people do to help stop air pollution and make the air safer? People can plant more trees. Trees can take away polluted air and help give fresh air. People can find a safer way to burn things. People can drive their cars less. People can make a difference.

Name _____

☞ Write your answers to these air pollution questions.

1. What does air pollution do to the air?

_____

_____

_____

2. Tell two things that cause air pollution.

_____

_____

_____

_____

3. Tell two ways people can help stop air pollution.

_____

_____

_____

_____

Draw a picture to show how you can help stop pollution.

Name _____

Sing a Song

☞ Read the words for each song. Find the correct word for each square. Cut it out. Glue it in the square.

The Wheels on the Bus

The wheels on the bus go round and round,

round and round,

round and round.

The wheels on the bus go round and

all through the town.

The people on the bus go up and down,

up and down,

up and down.

The people on the bus go up and

all through the ⬚ .

town

down

round

Name _____

Twinkle, Twinkle

Twinkle, twinkle little star,

How I wonder what you 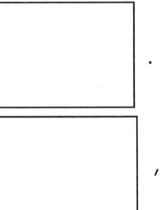 !

Up above the world so high,

Like a diamond in the [   ] .

Twinkle, twinkle little [   ] ,

How I wonder what you are!

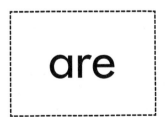
are

star

sky

Queen for a Day

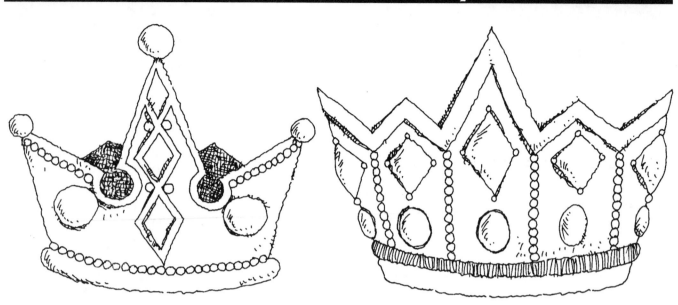

"The play is tomorrow. Are you ready?" Danielle asked Ima.

"I'm ready. I'm glad we get to practice while we wear our costumes," said Ima.

Danielle put on her crown. The colorful stones shone brightly. They matched her long red queen's robe.

Ima put on her crown. She tugged at her purple queen's robe. "I think this robe is too small," she said.

"My robe fits just right," said Danielle.

"Queens, come to the stage with your costumes on," said Mr. Jimenez.

Danielle and Ima dashed to the stage together.

Name _____

☞ How are Danielle and Ima alike and different? Circle Yes or No to answer each question.

1. Danielle and Ima are both queens in the play.   Yes No

2. Danielle and Ima both wear crowns.   Yes No

3. Danielle and Ima wear robes of different colors.   Yes No

4. Danielle's robe and Ima's robe fit the same.   Yes No

Draw a picture to show Danielle and Ima on the stage.

I Can Do It!

"We're going to enter the baking contest," said Inez. "We need one more person on our team. Ricardo, will you be on our team?"

"You know me," said Ricardo. "I'm not good at contests. I won't be able to do anything right."

"But you bake the best cake. Please be on our team."

"Maybe just this once," said Ricardo.

At the contest, everyone helped. Everything was mixed in the bowl. "Time to put it in the pan," said Inez. She turned around quickly. Bam! The bowl fell off the table. All the mix oozed out onto the floor.

"What will we do?" asked Inez. Her eyes grew wide. "Help, Ricardo. You're the only one who can mix it right. Please help."

Ricardo took a deep breath. His hands shook. "If you need me, I can do it," he said. Ricardo mixed everything in the bowl. He moved fast!

After the contest, Ricardo said to his friends, "I guess I can do things right. I'm glad we were in the contest together."

☞ **Write in the cakes below. Tell what happens in the beginning, middle, and end of the story.**

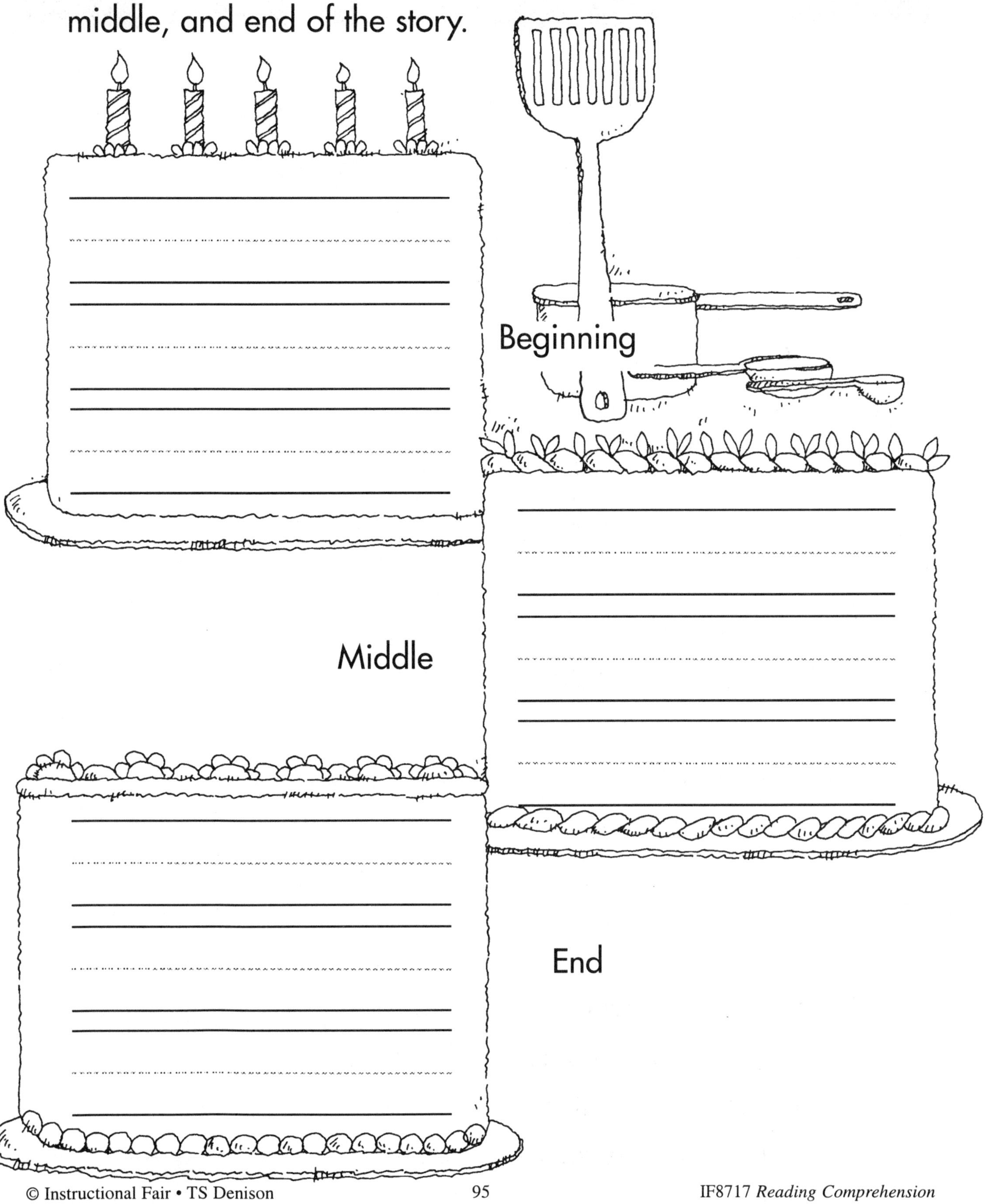

Beginning

Middle

End

Name _____

Where the Wild Things Live

What do the camel, the polar bear, the monkey, and the whale have in common? They're all mammals. But each of these mammals lives in a different climate. The camel lives in places that are dry and hot. The polar bear lives in icy cold, snowy places. The monkey lives in jungles that are hot and wet. And the whale lives in the ocean. It must live in water to stay alive.

☞ Tell how the camel, whale, monkey, and polar bear are alike.

_____

. . . .

_____

Each of these animals lives in a different climate. Draw a line from the animal to its climate.

camel	hot and wet
whale	hot and dry
polar bear	icy cold and snowy
monkey	ocean

Draw a picture to show each of these animals in the correct climate.

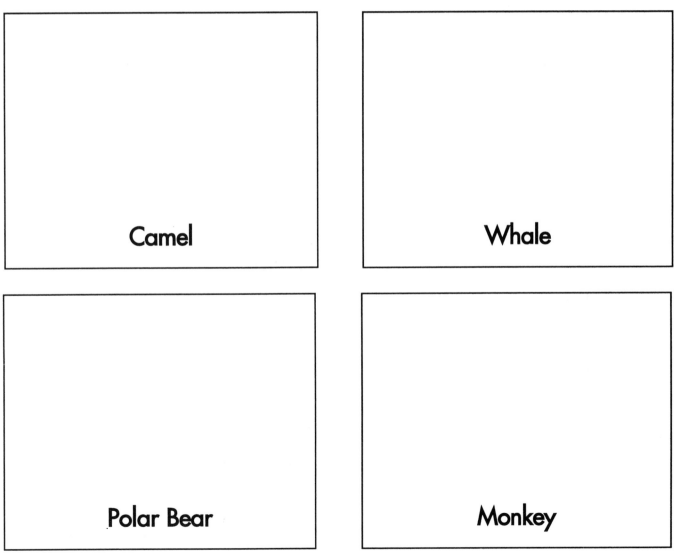

Camel

Whale

Polar Bear

Monkey

Spider

☞ Unscramble the words in the web. Write the correct unscrambled word above each picture.

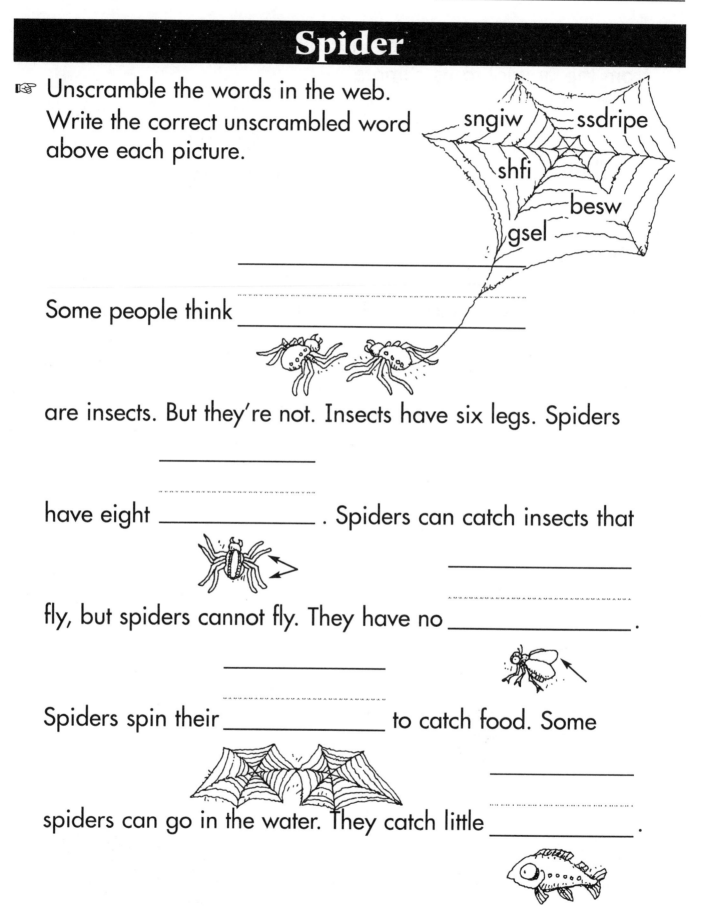

sngiw   ssdripe

shfi

besw

gsel

_____

Some people think _____

are insects. But they're not. Insects have six legs. Spiders

_____

have eight _____ . Spiders can catch insects that

_____

fly, but spiders cannot fly. They have no _____ .

_____

Spiders spin their _____ to catch food. Some

_____

spiders can go in the water. They catch little _____ .

On the Go!

It's spring! It's time for the big picnic.
But how do all the animals get there?
Carla Caterpillar crawls. Bubba Butterfly
flies. Freida Fish swims. Bertha Bee flies.
Wanda Wolf walks. Fred Frog hops.
Andrew Ant walks. Barsha Bunny hops.
Willy Worm crawls. Sasi Sea Horse swims.

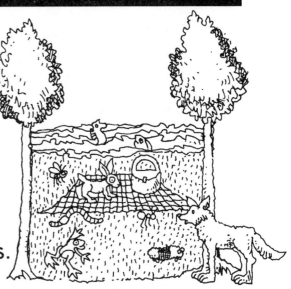

☞ How does each animal get to the picnic? Cut out the pictures
below. Glue them in the correct places.

Walks	Crawls	Hops	Flies	Swims

Name _____

Wah Chang

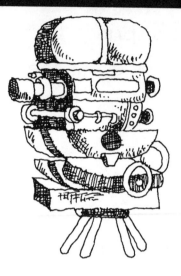

Wah Chang loved to draw. He drew pictures of cowboys when he was only three! Wah studied hard to learn more about art. By the time Wah was eight, he was showing his art work in art shows. People read about him in the newspaper.

Something very sad happened when Wah was eleven. His mother passed away. Wah was so very sad. But he gathered his strength and went on.

Wah worked for Walt Disney Studios when he was still young. He worked on movies, such as "Pinocchio" and "Bambi." Then Wah got very sick. He had polio. Some people who had polio died. Some were never able to walk again. But Wah worked long and hard. He was able to walk with special braces on his legs.

Wah continued to work on special effects. He worked for many films and television shows, such as "Star Trek." Even though he had many hard times, Wah Chang always worked to bring joy to others.

☞ Circle words from the Word Bank that tell about
Wah Chang.

Word Bank

kind	artist	lazy
hard worker	talented	worry
mean	never stopped trying	

In your own Word Bank, write words that tell about you.
Then, use those words to write sentences about yourself.

Word Bank

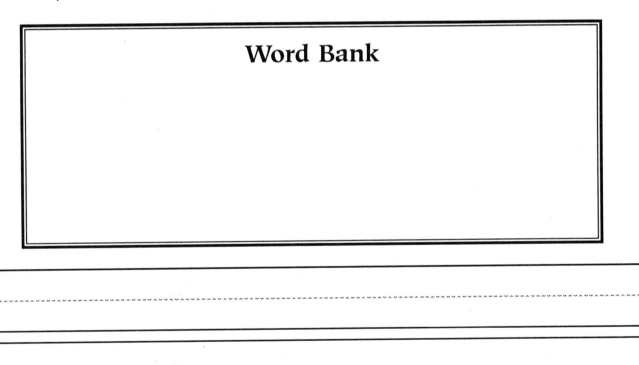

Name _____

So Many Places

☞ Read each story. Draw a line to the picture that shows the time and place for each story.

"Good morning, Mom," said Jaleel, as he raced down the stairs. "What time do we leave for vacation? I can hardly wait!"

"The lake is the best!" said Anais. She leaned against a tree. "I really like it when the sun starts to go down. I'm ready to tell scary stories."

The submarine moved deep in the ocean. Reggie saw fish and an octopus outside the window. He looked at his watch. It's so dark down here, it does not seem like four o'clock, he thought.

"Brrrr! It's so cold here on top of the mountain in the middle of the night." Shay pulled her hat down over her ears. Soon it would be time to go back down the mountain.

☞ # Choose one of the settings from page 102. Write your own story in that setting. Draw a scene from your story below.

What Do They Grow?

☞ Write the correct word on each line.

Who grows grapes? Grace grows grapes.

Who grows green beans?

_____

Grant _____ green beans.

Who grows grain?

_____

Greta grows _____ .

_____

Who eats Grace's _____ ,

_____

and Grant's _____ ,

_____

and Greta's _____ ?

A greedy green grasshopper eats them all!

Name _____

Points

Points on the needles,
Points on the nails,
Points on the starfish,
Points on the sails.

Points on the roofs,
Points on the bee,
Points on the playground,
Points for me!

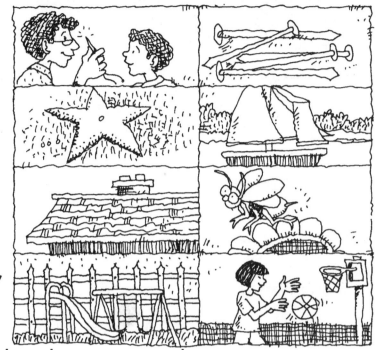

☞ In your own words, tell what the poem is about.

_____

....

_____

_____

~~~~~~

_____

How are the points in the last line of the poem different from
the other points in the poem?

_____

....

_____

Which of the points in the
poem is your favorite
kind? Draw a picture to
show your favorite.

Family Help

"Help me!" yelled Papa Squirrel. "I cannot walk. I cannot run." Papa Squirrel lay on the ground. A cat tiptoed nearby.

"I will help!" yelled Brother Squirrel. He ran down the tree. Brother Squirrel tried to lift Papa. "Papa, you are too heavy for me," said Brother Squirrel. Brother Squirrel ran back up the tree. "Papa needs help!" cried Brother Squirrel to Grandma Squirrel.

Grandma and Brother raced down the tree. "We will help you!" they yelled. "Papa, you are still too heavy for us." Brother looked up to the top of the tree. "Come down," Brother called to Sister Squirrel. She zoomed down the tree.

Brother and Grandma and Sister Squirrel used their paws and noses to push Papa. "Papa, you are not too heavy for us," said Brother and Grandma and Sister Squirrel. They pushed Papa up the tree. All the squirrels were safe.

☞ Write about the story. Tell what happens in the beginning, middle, and end of the story.

Beginning

Middle

End

_____

_____

_____

_____

_____

_____

_____

_____

_____

_____

_____

_____

_____

Think of a story you would like to tell. Plan the beginning, middle, and end. Write the story on another sheet of paper.

Beginning	Middle	End

Farm or Beach?

"Let's plan our trip!" said Lana. "I want to go to see Aunt Linda. She lives at the beach!"

"I want to go to see Grandma," said Sammy. "Grandma lives on the farm!"

"Both are fun trips," said Lana. "Let's go to the beach! We can swim in the ocean."

"Let's go to the farm!" said Sammy. "We can milk the cows!"

"Let's go to the beach!" said Lana. "We can build sand castles. We can catch crabs."

"Let's go to the farm!" said Sammy.

"We can see the baby chicks. We can feed the pigs."

"Let's go to the beach!" said Lana. "We can ride on a boat. We can go fishing. We can collect shells."

"Let's go to the farm!" said Sammy. "We can ride on the tractor. We can dig up potatoes. We can get the eggs."

"We can do both!" said Lana. "Let's go to the beach to see Aunt Linda. Then we'll take Aunt Linda to see Grandma. We can do it all. And we can do it together!"

☞ **How would a trip to the farm and a trip to the beach be alike?**

_____

_____

_____

How are a trip to the farm and a trip to the beach different?

_____

_____

_____

Cut out the pictures. On another sheet of paper, draw a beach and farm scene. Glue the pictures in the correct scenes.

Name _____

What Will They Do?

☞ Read each story. Circle the correct answer.

Joshua wants to be an actor more than anything. He takes acting classes. He has been in plays. He has a chance to be in another play. He has to try out this afternoon. The phone rings. Joshua's friend is calling. He wants Joshua to come over this afternoon.

1. What will Joshua do?

    A. Joshua will go to his friend's house.
    B. Joshua will go to try out for the play.

Dalia has been racing on her bicycle after school for two years. She is tired of bicycle races. She wants to try something new. Dalia's teacher asks Dalia to swim on the swim team after school.

2. What will Dalia do?

    A. Dalia will swim.
    B. Dalia will race on her bicycle.

All animals have to eat to stay alive. Squirrels eat nuts. Whales eat sea plants and animals. Other animals eat many different things. A squirrel is hungry. It sees sea plants and nuts.

3. What will the squirrel do?

   A. The squirrel will eat the nuts.
   B. The squirrel will eat the sea plants.

Lucy loves her uncle. He is very special to her. Lucy wants to buy a birthday present for her uncle. He likes fishing, and she wants to buy him a fishing book. But she doesn't have enough money. Lucy saves her money for two months. Finally, she has enough money for the book.

4. What will Lucy do?

   A. Lucy will buy herself a new video game.
   B. Lucy will buy a fishing book for her uncle.

Party Mask

Ranita Raccoon wanted to go to a party. But she needed a mask. So she went to Brian Bear's Party Shop. "Why do you need a mask?" asked Brian Bear. "You already have one."

"Not really," Ranita answered. "All raccoons have a mask like mine. Will you help me find something different?"

"Sure," answered Brian. "Tell me about the mask you'd like to wear."

"I'd like a really big mask," said Ranita. "One with feathers. I'd like it to be bright and shiny. And I'd like it to have a flag with two circles and two triangles."

"I can see you really know what you're looking for," said Brian. "Wait here. I'll be back."

☞ **Help Brian choose the mask for Ranita. Circle the correct mask.**

Draw a mask you would like to wear to a party.

Name _____

Ocean Food

People eat many things that come from the ocean. You've probably eaten several kinds of fish. Some people like shrimp. Others like clams and lobsters. People even eat plants from the ocean. Seaweed is one ocean plant some people like to eat. You may have eaten seaweed. One kind of seaweed is used to make ice cream!

☞ What is Ocean Food mostly about? Circle the correct answer.

A. People eat some kinds of plants from the ocean.

B. Some people like shrimp.

C. People eat many things that come from the ocean.

D. People like to eat clams.

Draw ocean animals and plants in the scene below.

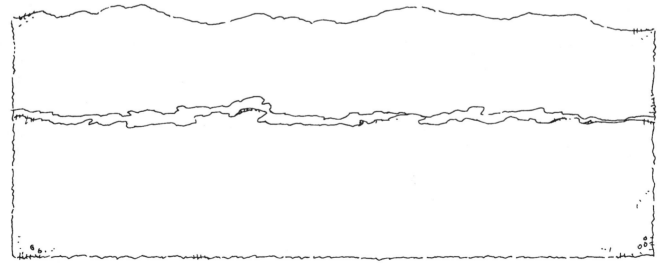

Name _____

Feathered Friends

What is alike about all birds? They all have feathers. No birds have scales. What is different about birds? Some birds live in caves. They can fly in the dark. And they still know where they are going. Most birds live outside caves. They like to soar in the sky.

☞ Write the correct word in each blank.

1. _____ birds can fly in the dark.

2. _____ birds have feathers.

3. _____ birds have scales.

4. _____ birds live outside caves.

| Most | All | No | Some |

Finish the Line Rhyme

☞ Read each rhyme.
Circle the picture that shows what happens next.

Rover runs up.

Rover runs down.

Rover runs all around the town.

Rover runs up.

Rover runs down.

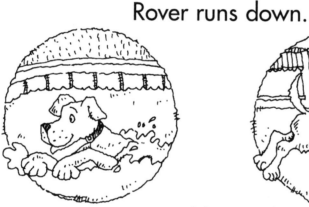

Kim likes to fly

high in the sky.

It's vacation time!

Name _____

I read every chance I get.

I love to grab a book.

It's one place where I love to go

To look and look and look.

Rain has fallen

all week long.

Must we stay inside?

Maybe we could go outside

and take a little ride.

On the Coast

Los Angeles and New York are alike because they are both cities. Many movies and television shows are filmed in both cities. Los Angeles is on the West Coast. New York is on the East Coast. The weather stays warm in Los Angeles during the winter. The weather gets very cold in New York during the winter. Both cities can be fun to visit.

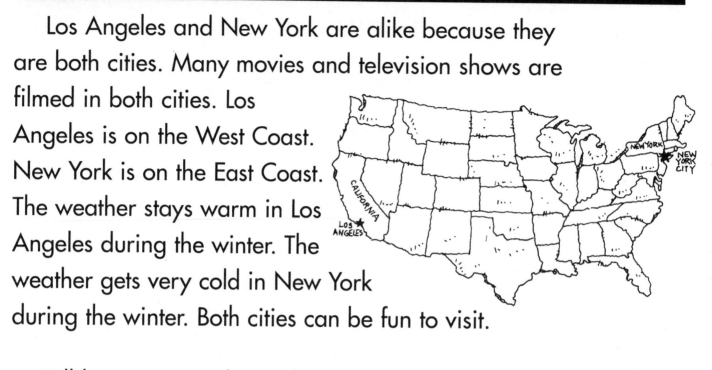

☞ Tell how Los Angeles and New York are alike and different by writing about them in the circles.

Los Angeles   **New York City**

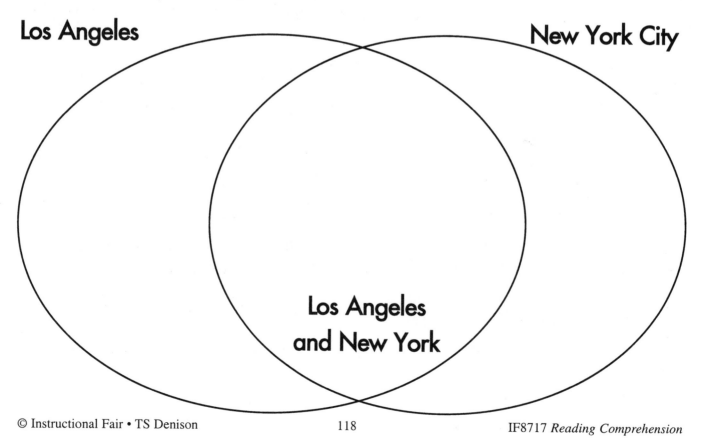

Los Angeles
and New York

Answer Key

Jan's Job 4
(sequencing)

| 3 | 4 | 1 | 2 |

Rain, Rain, Go Away 5
(inferencing)

No

No

Yes

No

Ouches in Our Pouches 6–7
(drawing conclusions)

Soft baby joey goes in the mother
  kangaroo's pouch.

Egg-stra Safe! 8
(cause and effect)

People hurried to see because Humpty hit
  his head.

Humpty wasn't hurt because he wore a
  helmet.

Humpty fell because his horse tripped.

Taking Care of Fifi 9
(classifying)

Below Ling's picture:
  dog food, dog biscuits, dog dish

Below Juan's picture:
  dog brush, dog shampoo, large tub

What Makes You Special? 10
(picture clues)

Ziri: boy feeding cat

Josefina: girl kicking soccer ball

Dana: girl putting can into recycling bin

Ahmed: boy looking at sheet music

Wah: boy sitting next to sculpture handling
  clay

Pictures and stories will vary.

Go! 11
(summarizing)

Answers will vary but student might be surprised that the last item has no wheels.

And Then What Happens? 12–13
(predicting)

1. boy playing basketball with grandmother
2. window basket of flowers with water
   overflowing
3. boy and grandfather eating fruit salad
4. girl comforting younger brother

Trunks and Necks 14–15
(compare and contrast)

In elephant circle: long trunk, gray, picks up
  peanuts

In giraffe circle: long neck, yellow, long legs

In overlap: mammal, an animal, looks for
  food

Fishing for Light 16
(sequencing)

3

4

2

1

Rhyme Time 17
(cloze)

crown

fiddle

spoon

Bink! Bonk! 18–19
(analyzing character)

Bink: rude, careless, mean

Bonk: kind, careful, doesn't give up

Sentences will vary but should show understanding of the characters.

Agree to Disagree 20
(fact or opinion)

1. O   2. O

3. F   4. F

5. O   6. O

Riddle Around 21
(following directions)

1. basketball rim

2. Drawings will vary but should reflect
understanding of position word *over*.

3. Drawings will vary but should reflect
understanding of *under*.

4. Drawings will vary but should reflect
understanding of *behind*.

Whose Shoes? 22–23
(reading for details)

Brice: triangles

Mohammed: shells

Lila: circles

Avi: stripes

Kate: rockets

Resa: stars

In the Rain Forest 24–25
(reading a graph)

1. tree frog

2. monkey and jaguar

3. snake

4. ant

Reduce, Reuse, Recycle 26–27
(classifying)

Plastic: plastic juice carton, disposable
plastic food container

Paper: newspaper, advertisement

Glass: jar, glass milk bottle

Cans: soft-drink can, vegetable can

Go Anywhere! 28–29
(following directions)

Map: Draw line down First Street from
school to A Street. Go left on A Street to
Second Street. Turn right on Second
Street. Go all the way down Second to
the library.

1. Lon is waiting at the library.

2. Answers will vary but should reflect
knowledge that books can take people
many places.

Flying the Friendly Skies 30
(compare and contrast)

First Planes: room for only one person; no cover for pilot's seat; dirt blew into pilot's face; no seat belts; pilots sometimes fell out of planes

Planes Today: room for many people; planes have covers; pilots don't fall out; dirt doesn't blow into pilot's face; planes have seat belts

Drawings will vary.

It's a Fact! Or Is It? 31
(fact or opinion)

1. F
2. O
3. O
4. F

Answers will vary but should reflect knowledge of distinction between fact and opinion.

Team Work 32–33
(main idea)

1. animal teams
2. big fish
3. big bugs
4. safe

Tornado! 34
(critical thinking)

1. Answers will vary but should reflect knowledge of safety issues, such as windows bursting and flying objects coming into house.

2. Answers will vary but should reflect knowledge that bathtub is a safe place to be during a tornado.

Under the Sea 35
(following directions)

Stage should show the following: starfish near table wearing purple bracelet; crab at top of stairs wearing gold crown; Sea horse near mirror wearing red bow; electric eel wrapped around pole.

Robbie's Job 36–37
(analyzing character)

1. doctor
2. teacher
3. lawyer
4. vet

Answers will vary but should show support for decision through information from reading selection. Children will likely choose lawyer.

Way to Grow! 38
(predicting)

Sean is the happy-faced boy. His garden should look healthy with lots of plants growing.

Rob is the sad-faced boy. His garden should look unhealthy with droopy plants.

Answers will vary but should reflect knowledge of items that grow in a garden.

I Can! .39
(inferencing)
1. bee
2. dog
3. kind
4. happy
Drawings should show bee and dog.

Moon Walk 40
(reading for details)
1. No
2. Yes
3. Yes
4. No
5. Yes
Drawings will vary.

Pet Match 41
(critical thinking)
Jeremy: horse
Adrian: hamster
Kenya: dog
Bob: pig
Ashley: cat

Clowning Around 42–43
(sequencing)
boy blowing out candle
clown blowing up balloons
clown holding balloon dog
clown playing harmonica
clown disappearing in smoke

Yum! Yum! 44–45
(inferencing)
1. lemonade

2. cake
3. cookies
4. vegetable salad
Drawings will vary.

Hats Off! 46–47
(classifying)
Chart will contain two western hats, three
    baseball hats, one clown hat, and two
    chef hats.

A Horse of a Different Color . . .48–49
(reading for details)
Will's horse is blue.
Noreen's horse is green.
Fred's horse is red.
Anna's horse is orange.
Kwan's horse is purple.

It's Cold Outside! 50–51
(inferencing)
1. No
2. No
3. Yes
4. No
Drawings will vary but should show grand-
    mother and girl throwing snowballs.

Could This Really Happen? 52–53
(reality or fantasy)
1. could not
2. could
3. could
4. could not

Long Ago 54
(generalizing)
1. Many
2. All
3. No
4. Some
Drawings will vary.

Talk to the Animals 55
(summarizing)
Answers will vary but should be short and
in child's own words.

Who's Afraid? 56–57
(analyzing plot)
Beginning: Sandra invites Kim to the beach.
Middle: Sandra gets hurt.
End: Kim helps Sandra.

Where and When? 58–59
(recognizing setting)
1. at midnight in a mouse home
2. early morning at school
3. in 3010, in a spaceship

Up, Up, and Away 60
(context clues)
floated
fell
popped
caught

Paul's Pasta 61
(sequencing)
3
5
1
4
2

Ocean View 62–63
(compare and contrast)
Flying fish: live near top of ocean, have short
tails, can jump
Both: live in ocean, can swim
Rat-tail fish: live deep in the ocean, have
long tails, cannot jump

Planets and Moons 64–65
(reading a graph)
1. Mars
2. Mercury and Venus
3. Pluto
4. Jupiter

Could This Be Real? 66–67
(reality or fantasy)
1. No
2. Yes
3. Yes
4. No
5. Yes
Pictures will vary but should reflect understanding of distinction between reality
and fantasy.

Picnic Poster 68–69
(reading for details)

Where: Silas Park

When: Sunday, May 25th

Bring: food

Poster should include Tad's signature.

Ring Around the Moon 70–71
(sequencing)

1. child talking to smiling Pluto
2. child talking to sad-faced Mars
3. child jetting away from Saturn with ring
4. smiling Mars

Too Big 72–73
(analyzing character)

1. sad dog
2. Answers will vary but should reflect that Barker feels sad.
3. happy dog
4. Answers will vary but should reflect that Barker feels happy and needed.
5. Answers will vary but should reflect knowledge that Barker's feelings changed because Barker did something important; something that made her feel special.

Time to Camp! 74–75
(main idea and details)

Main idea: It's important to prepare for a camping trip.

Supporting details:

Bring marshmallows for a tasty treat.

You'll need a flashlight.

Your shoes should feel good on your feet.

Elephant Gardens 76
(following directions)

Picture should show blue pond, gray elephant, purple short flowers, orange tall flowers, a green circle around the vegetable garden, pencil marks indicating water coming from elephant's trunk and spewing over gardens.

Guiding the Way 77
(analyzing character)

Delia: kind, helpful, loving, caring

Answers will vary but should reflect understanding of the love and help the dog and human give to each other.

The Earth Is a Puzzle 78–79
(summarizing)

Answers will vary but should be in child's own words and should reflect important points in selection.

Earth "puzzle" should match Earth illustration.

Through the Hoop 80–81
(critical thinking)

Scoreboard should show total of 8 points for each team.

1. No
2. No
3. Yes

Building Up 82–83
(reading a graph)

1. group D
2. group A
3. group D
4. group B
5. group A

What Would You Expect? 84–85
(predicting)

1. Circles will ripple out into the water.
2. sandwiches and popcorn
3. The puddles were gone.
4. Chin will do well.

Earthquake! 86
(generalizing)

1. Many
2. All
3. No
4. Some
5. Most

Up in the Sky, Down on the Ground 87
(main idea)

1. birds that can't fly
2. small
3. like flippers

Pollution Solution 88–89
(cause and effect)

1. Pollution makes the air unsafe.
2. Smoke and cars cause air pollution.
3. Plant more trees; find a safer way to burn things; and drive their cars less.

Drawings will vary but should reflect knowledge of solutions to pollution.

Sing a Song 90–91
(cloze)

1. round
2. down
3. town
4. are
5. sky
6. star

Queen for a Day 92–93
(compare and contrast)

1. Yes
2. Yes
3. Yes
4. No

Drawings will vary but should show Danielle in red robe that fits and Ima in purple robe that is too small.

I Can Do It! 94–95
(analyzing plot)

Beginning: Inez asks Ricardo to enter baking contest.

Middle: The cake mix is ready, but spills.

End: Ricardo mixes the new cake and is happy he entered the contest.

Where the Wild Things Live 96–97
(compare and contrast)

All these animals are mammals.

Camel: hot and dry

Whale: ocean

Polar bear: icy cold and snowy

Monkey: hot and wet

Drawings will vary but should show appropriate habitats.

Spider .98
(picture clues)
spiders
legs
wings
webs
fish

On the Go! 99
(classifying)
Walks: wolf, ant
Crawsl: caterpillar, worm
Hops: frog, bunny
Flies: butterfly, bee
Swims: fish, sea horse

Wah Chang 100–101
(analyzing character)
hard worker, kind, talented, artist, never
    stopped trying
Word Banks and sentences will vary.

So Many Places 102–103
(recognizing setting)
Paragraph one: boy racing down stairs early
    in morning
Paragraph two: sunset on lake near forest
Paragraph three: submarine
Paragraph four: mountaintop
Stories will vary but should reflect knowl-
    edge of setting.

What Do They Grow? 104
(cloze)
1. grows
2. grain
3. grapes
4. green beans
5. grain

Points 105
(critical thinking)
Answers will vary but should be short and in
    child's own words. Answers should reflect
    understanding of difference in meaning of
    points at end of the poem.
Drawings will vary.

Family Help 106–107
(analyzing plot)
Beginning: Papa falls out of tree.
Middle: Different squirrels try to help.
End: Three squirrels work together to push
    Papa up tree, and he is safe.
Stories will vary but should reflect familiarity
    with plot.

Farm or Beach? 108–109
(compare and contrast)
Alike: Both would be fun trips.
Farm: collecting eggs, riding on tractor, dig-
    ging up potatoes, feeding pigs, watching
    chicks, milking cows
Beach: swimming in ocean, catching crabs,
    riding on boat, building sand castles, fish-
    ing, collecting shells

What Will They Do? 110–111
(predicting)
1. Joshua will go to try out for the play.
2. Dalia will swim.
3. The squirrel will eat the nuts.
4. Lucy will buy a fishing book for her uncle.

Party Mask 112–113
(reading for details)
Correct mask: big mask with feather, sequins, and flag with two circles and two triangles
Drawings will vary.

Ocean Food 114
(main idea)
C. People eat many things that come from the ocean.
Drawings will vary but should include fish, shrimp, clams, lobsters, and seaweed.

Feathered Friends 115
(generalizing)
1. Some
2. All
3. No
4. Most

Finish the Line Rhyme 116–117
(predicting)
1. dog running in town
2. girl in airplane
3. boy at library
4. children in boat

On the Coast 118
(compare and contrast)
Los Angeles: on West Coast; weather stays warm in winter
New York: on East Coast; weather gets very cold in winter
Both: cities, movies and television shows filmed in both, fun to visit